W9-AQY-594

BIG BOOK OF
Whittle Fun

31 Simple Projects You Can Make with a Knife, Branches & Other Found Wood

Chris Lubkemann

Fox Chapel
PUBLISHING

DON'T SHOOT PEOPLE OR ANIMALS

Some of the projects in this book can launch objects through the air or shoot objects at a fast pace. Be extremely careful not to aim at any people or animals. If you want to shoot at something, line up some action figures or cans and bottles. You can even create your own wooden target using some of the skills you learn in this book.

© 2012 by Chris Lubkemann and Fox Chapel Publishing Company, Inc., East Petersburg, PA.

Big Book of Whittle Fun is an original work, first published in 2012 by Fox Chapel Publishing Company, Inc. No part of this book may be duplicated for resale or distribution under any circumstances. Any such copying is a violation of copyright law.

ISBN 978-1-56523-520-5

Library of Congress Cataloging-in-Publication Data

Lubkemann, Ernest C.
  The Big Book of Whittle Fun / Chris Lubkemann.
      p. cm.
  Includes index.
  ISBN 978-1-56523-520-5
  1. Wood-carving. I. Title.
  TT199.7.L82238 2012
  736'.4--dc23

7-2 1-15 H

      2011037937

To learn more about the other great books from Fox Chapel Publishing, or to find a retailer near you, call toll-free 800-457-9112 or visit us at *www.FoxChapelPublishing.com*.

Note to Authors: We are always looking for talented authors to write new books. Please send a brief letter describing your idea to Acquisition Editor, 1970 Broad Street, East Petersburg, PA 17520.

Printed in China
Fourth printing

Because carving wood and other materials inherently includes the risk of injury and damage, this book cannot guarantee that creating the projects in this book is safe for everyone. For this reason, this book is sold without warranties or guarantees of any kind, expressed or implied, and the publisher and the author disclaim any liability for any injuries, losses, or damages caused in any way by the content of this book or the reader's use of the tools needed to complete the projects presented here. The publisher and the author urge all readers to thoroughly review each project and to understand the use of all tools before beginning any project.t

Dedication

This book is lovingly dedicated to my six grandchildren—Sophia, Ava, Katarina, Isaac, Kennedy, and Riley—all of whom have inherited little bits of my carvings over the years, and do seem to appreciate them. Well, maybe not Riley, yet. At the time of this writing, she was only four days old! Don't worry, Riley, you'll get your share too!

Acknowledgements

While I consider myself at least fairly proficient in my knowledge and experience with what is explained in this book as related to wood and the use of a pocketknife, I can't claim expertise in all aspects of history, games, and camp recipes. For these super-interesting little additions scattered throughout the book and which add so much to it, all credit goes to Katie and the Fox Chapel Publishing team.

About the Author

A child of missionaries, Chris Lubkemann grew up in the forests of Brazil and Peru, where sawing, planing, hammering, and building were a part of daily life. He quickly developed an appreciation for wood and entertained himself—and others—by handcrafting rafts, tree houses, traps, and slingshots from scrap wood. Since that time, he has continued to integrate his woodworking skills with good old-fashioned fun.

Chris's first writing on whittling appeared in 1972 in the form of published notes, which have since been produced in both English and Portuguese. Since that time, Chris has produced three books: *Whittling Twigs and Branches*, *The Little Book of Whittling*, and *Tree Craft: 35 Rustic Wood Projects That Bring the Outdoors In*. For many years, Chris was a regular contributor to *Chip Chats* magazine. His work has been featured in *Wood Carving Illustrated* magazine and on the DIY network. He has carved some of the world's smallest branch carvings, and his smallest branch rooster was given a Guinness World Record Certificate in 1981.

Currently, Chris demonstrates whittling as the resident woodcarver at the Amish Farm and House in Lancaster, Pennsylvania.

Preface

Some time ago, when Alan Giagnocavo and I were talking on the upstairs floor of Fox Chapel Publishing's book warehouse, he slipped a sentence into his conversation; something to the effect of, "Chris, why don't you come up with another series of projects to make a sequel book to *The Little Book of Whittling*?" (I had just finished writing *Tree Craft: 35 Rustic Wood Projects that Bring the Outdoors In*.)

I responded quite quickly, as I recall, "Alan, I really think my idea tank is quite empty at this point!"

"Well, just keep it in mind."

When I went home, I told my wife, Sheri, both about Alan's question and my response. "Hah!" she said. "You'll come up with plenty of ideas. There's no way you're done!" (I'm sure I'm paraphrasing, but that was the gist of her reaction.)

To make a long story short, that night, while I was half asleep and half awake, ideas started popping into my head right and left—and in the middle, too. By morning, the project list exceeded twenty, and they kept coming. I called the folks at Fox back, turned in a proposal, made a bunch of samples, and, rather surprising (to *me* at least), here's the book.

Here's hoping the ideas that are described and illustrated in the following pages will provide lots of fun to many who try them, and will "prime the pump" for many more ideas to come.

— Chris

Discover the Joy of Whittling!

13 SELECTING THE BEST KNIFE.

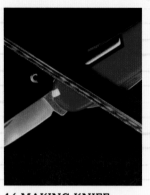

14 MAKING KNIFE MODIFICATIONS.

17 THE BASIC CUTTING STROKES.

20 CREATIVE AND DECORATIVE PROJECTS.

Helpful tips and fun facts.

The Little Book of Whittling was filled with helpful camping tips, fun facts, and interesting information, and you'll find this book continues the tradition. Look for these helpful blue boxes to discover delicious recipes, new games, and to learn a little extra about the projects you're whittling. Also, don't turn a page without looking at the bottom for some little facts and tips. These tidbits are meant to remind you of the fun and relaxation whittling should provide. Share some of your favorites with your friends and family.

Table of Contents

Getting Started

The Little Book of Whittling, besides being smaller than the average woodcarving book (easier to carry around and stick in a backpack), describes and illustrates nineteen projects, most of which are also on the small side.

The *Big Book of Whittle Fun* follows the same format and basic theme—a small book with generally small, and *quick*, projects. (We've even added some new fun facts and camping tips). While some of these projects are different scale variations of projects in several of my other books, most are new and different.

Because we're still dealing with wood and knives and a few other tools, and some who are reading *this* book don't have access to the others, let me repeat a few basic bits of information, some suggestions, and maybe even several instructions that apply across the board as related to whittling, carving, and woodworking in general.

At my shop in Lancaster, Pennsylvania, I have visitors from all over the world. Just for fun, here is my main, all-important rule for whittling that I try to get across to folks in a few of the many languages I encounter:

Assurez-vous que votre canif est bien aiguisé.   (French)

Achten Sie darauf, daß das Messer scharf ist.   (German)

Asegúrese de que la navaja esté afilada. (Spanish)

确保你的刀锋利 (Chinese)

Убедитесь, что ваш нож острый.   (Russian)

O seu canivete tem que estar mesmo bem afiado!   (Portuguese)

Hãy nhớ lưỡi dao phải thật bén!   (Vietnamese)

And to make sure the rest of the readers get the idea, let me express this rule a few more ways:

- Make sure your knife is really sharp!
- Don't try carving with a knife that isn't sharp!
- You'll be a lot more successful at carving and have a lot more fun if your knife is sharp!

Outside of these rules, it wouldn't hurt to be reminded that the order followed in the step-by-step instructions generally follows a certain logical sequence, and **if you stick with that order,** the project is likely to come out well and you won't end up painting yourself into some corner that's hard to carve yourself out of without messing up.

A good knife is pretty much all you need to start whittling.
Materials for your projects can be found almost anywhere.

About Knives And Sharpening

Since that summer day in 1966 in Glendale Springs, North Carolina, when I hatched my first branch rooster, my primary tool for the majority of my whittling and carving projects has been a two-bladed pocketknife. As I recall, my first knife was a brown-handled, two-bladed Barlow made by Imperial in Providence, Rhode Island. That $2.95 (maybe less) knife from one of the local Ashe County country stores actually helped me pay my way through my senior year of college! And, if my memory serves me right, that same old knife helped keep paying the bills for several more years.

While I've happily used a fair number of other pocketknives since then, the knife that has been my mainstay for the past decade or so has been the Victorinox Swiss Army Tinker. Actually, I started using it more or less by default. The knife I had been working with for a number of years developed an irreversible weakness, and being the super-conservative spender that I am (I believe "skinflint" is too strong a word), instead of springing for a new knife, I decided to try the Swiss Army Tinker someone had given me. I made a couple modifications to it and began carving. And here I am, all these years later, still using the Tinker. In fact, I just pulled it out of my pocket.

True, after carving thousands and thousands of projects, it did end up on the disabled list for a while, though through no fault of its own. Very stupidly, I used the Phillips-head screwdriver on a screw that had way too much torque, and in the process I broke the spring inside the knife. Finally, at someone's suggestion, I sent the knife to the Victorinox U.S. headquarters to be repaired. Very nicely I threatened the manager of the repair department, warning her she could not simply replace my old knife with a new one. (I told her it would not be a problem to drive my giant "country pitching machine," which pitches baseballs accurately at 130 miles per hour (209 kilometers per hour) and can launch 500-foot (152-meter) home runs, all the way up to Connecticut.) But I also sent a copy of *Whittling Twigs and Branches*, the book my Tinker had helped produce, to her and the rest of the Victorinox staff.

Anyway, they couldn't have been nicer. They repaired the broken spring, put new scales on the knife, and even gave me a new toothpick. (I had lost the original.) All my well-used blades and other parts were still the same, and they even returned my beaten-up, well-worn scales. Needless to say, I am more than thrilled to have my very special, well-traveled, and super-productive knife back in my pocket...and hands!

What to look for in a good pocketknife

There are several things you will want out of your pocketknife. First, you'll want a knife with two blades: a small 1–1½" (25–38mm) blade and a large 2–2¼" (51–57mm) blade. The small blade will do most of the work. Second, you will need a knife with good steel. This means the blade sharpens well and holds an edge. Some carvers are down on stainless steel, but I've found there are some very good stainless steel blades out there. One reason I recommend the Victorinox Tinker (the Recruit and Hiker are good too) is I've been very satisfied with the steel. The knife is also easy to find and reasonably priced.

A final essential quality in a knife is a strong handle with a tight connection between the handle and blades.

You may already have a knife that meets these qualifications. Great! Use it. If you're a carver, you probably have a few fixed-blade carving knives. Of course these will work fine. Just don't try sticking them into your pocket!

A good knife has two blades —a small one and a large one—made of quality steel.

Making modifications

Before describing my rather primitive, but effective, sharpening system, let me share the two modifications I've made to my Tinker knife in order to make it most useful for the type of carving I do.

I'll walk you through the steps I take to transform a Victorinox Swiss Army Tinker into an ideal branch-carving pocketknife.

1. The Tinker as it comes from the box.

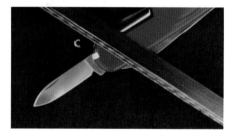

2. Remove the key ring and saw off the little tab that holds it. File off any sharp edges. (I remove this tab because it is located in exactly the wrong place if you're going to use the small blade a lot, especially the way you do in carving.)

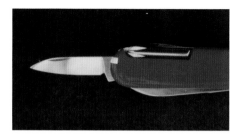

3. Taper the small blade top and bottom to bring the blade to a thinner point, which is much better for tighter turn cuts. Notice the difference between the small blades in Step 1 and Step 3. Now you'll have to resharpen and hone the small blade.

I might mention that the Victorinox Swiss Army knives are among the few pocketknives that I've found to be reasonably sharp right out of the box. However, I'm sure most carvers will want to fine-tune both blades to get the edge they find ideal.

And one further note: I would not recommend any knives with corkscrews, as the corkscrew makes for a very uncomfortable grip when working with the small blade. The Phillips screwdriver of the Tinker nestles quite nicely into the handle and doesn't bother you the way the corkscrew does.

Sharpening and Honing

If you've already read *The Little Book of Whittling*, you might recognize some of the tips in this section. I'm still using the same method, and, believe it or not, a number of the exact same little strips of wet-or-dry sandpaper mentioned in the first book. I think one of the little strips (or what's left of it) has been honing my knives for about twelve years. What grit was it when I started using it? I honestly can't remember. Right now the little grey spots that are left on it are probably somewhere around 10,000!

There are all kinds of methods and devices for sharpening knives. I will share with you my own very simple sharpening system, but feel free to experiment and find what works best for you.

Like any method or system, mine takes a little practice, but it does work, and I've been satisfied with it for quite a few years. The price is pretty good, too—practically nothing, after a very small initial investment.

If I'm starting out with a totally dull knife (even a new blade can be dull), I usually use my two-sided sharpening stone to get the process started—first the coarser surface and then the finer. (Most sharpening stones have two surfaces.) With the blade not quite flat against the stone, I use a circular motion followed up by several slicing motions. After this part, the blade is semi-sharp, but not yet ready for carving.

Then, I'll go to a series of little strips of wet-or-dry sandpaper or emery cloth—like the kind used on auto bodywork. The three grits I generally use are 320, 400, and 600 (the higher the number, the finer the grit). Some of my little beat-up sheets have been around for eight or ten years and are still working. They're virtually paper-smooth, but they still serve to polish the blade's edge.

Finally, I'll end up stropping (wiping) my blade on a piece of leather, usually with a little bit of stropping compound. For many years, I just used the rough backside of an old leather belt.

If I'm starting with a blade that only needs a touch of sharpening, I'll start with the finest grit of wet-or-dry sandpaper and finish with a few strops on the leather.

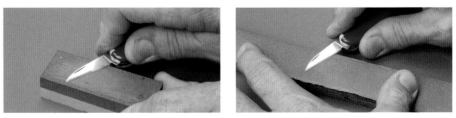

With the blade not quite flat, move your knife across the coarse side of a sharpening stone (left) using a circular motion. Then, make a few slicing motions across the stone. Don't lift or turn the blade as it goes across the stone. Flip to the finer (yellow) side and repeat. Then, repeat the process using wet-or-dry sandpaper on top of a block of wood (right), going through the grits from coarse to fine.

Other Tools And Supplies

Besides a good knife, there are a number of other tools and supplies you'll need in order to finish the projects in this book. No doubt you probably have several of them on hand.

Handsaw: A small one will work fine. I personally prefer the aggressive-toothed saws with twelve or fifteen teeth per inch. Another saw I enjoy very much is the Japanese pull saw. It's particularly useful for making the little slices called for in some of the projects. I didn't even know about this little saw until a number of years ago when my son Steve gave me one as a present. It sat around pretty much untouched for a while, but when I actually put it to use, *wow*, I was hooked. It's a great little tool. I've checked around, and both hardware stores and building supply stores carry them, so you shouldn't have any trouble finding one.

Electric drill and bits: Nothing special, just a simple drill and a variety of bits for wood.

Rotary tool: This is called for in the salt dipper spoons project (page 25). However, you might discover another use or two for it.

Woodburner: This is one of my favorite tools, and I use it constantly. About half of my total custom business involves burning people's names on little logs or pieces of milled wood. While the little burners you can buy at the average craft store will work on softer woods, they're not very practical if you want to do more serious woodburning. In my own opinion, a decent woodburner is definitely a good investment, and the most practical woodburner tip to get for the type of burning described in this book is the *writing* tip.

Sandpaper: Fine- to medium-grit.

Pencil and permanent markers: You will need a pencil for occasional drawing and marking, and permanent markers of various colors for coloring in some of the small woodburned designs you'll make.

Paints: For the projects in this book, acrylic paints will work fine.

Paintbrushes: Keep several small brushes on hand, ranging in size from #00 to #2. You also might want a few on hand that are a little bigger.

Clear finish: Many projects don't call for any finish at all, but others you might want to protect with a coat of polyurethane or a clear acrylic spray. Be *very careful* in your choice of finish for the branch rooster, for reasons that will be discussed when you reach that project.

Three Basic Cutting Strokes

There are several ways to cut with a knife. The three particular strokes described here are illustrated for right-handed carvers. Left-handers, of course, will reverse the hands, following a mirror image of the illustrations.

Straightaway cutting

This cut is good for removing a lot of wood or bark quickly. Hold the wood in your left hand, and using long, firm strokes, cut away from yourself with your right hand. I find that when I use this stroke my right wrist is pretty well locked, not bending during the cutting stroke.

Drawcutting

This technique involves placing the wood in your left hand and the knife in your right. Cut toward yourself (sort of like peeling an orange) with short strokes, using your right thumb as a brace against the wood. I find it helpful (and much safer) to keep my right thumb braced on my left thumb, not on top of the wood itself. That way, I don't run the risk of the blade coming up into my right thumb on its follow-through when it suddenly clears the end of the wood.

Thumbpushing

This particular stroke is extremely practical for small cuts where precise control is needed and you don't want to overcut. Hold the wood in the four fingers of your left hand, leaving your left thumb free. Grip the knife in your right hand, keeping your right thumb against the back of the blade. With your left thumb, push either the back of the blade or the back of your right thumb.

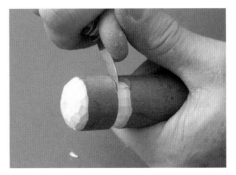

About Wood

While some of the projects in this book can be made with soft woods like seasoned dried white pine, or even basswood, I've generally recommended the use of hardwoods like birch, maple, cherry, holly, beech, various citrus woods, and even ironwood. Especially for the rooster project (page 73), you'll find using hardwood is definitely better. For most of the projects that call for twigs or branches, you'll want a wood that has a relatively small pith (the soft, spongy center). Also, so you won't be fighting constantly with a sticky knife and hands, avoid fresh pine or any other sappy wood.

For some of the following projects, the type of wood you use really isn't that important or critical. For others, however, the kind of wood can make quite a bit of difference. When wood choice is important I'll point that out.

Of course, the best way to determine the types of wood you like to work with is to experiment and practice. The following list includes just a few of my favorites.

Birch: Any variety of birch is excellent. I've never met a bad birch yet! The birches are among my all-time favorite woods.

Maple: There are quite a few varieties of maple, too. Some have a very small pith, and others have a large pith. For most projects, the smaller-pith variety works better. Just experiment. Any maple is worth trying. Swamp maple is one of my favorites.

Cherry: I've carved several kinds of cherry, both domesticated and wild. All are quite good.

Beech: I've found that beech can be a bit brittle, but if you're careful, it works fine.

Oak: There are many varieties of oak, and some are much better than others for certain projects. I've made some nice pieces from pin oak, live oak, and water oak. Red oak is not particularly good for most of these projects, because it tends to have a very open grain that's kind of wavy.

Holly: A very hard, close-grained wood that produces some beautiful pieces.

Orange, lemon, tangerine, grapefruit:
All of the citrus woods are good (except for the new, fast-growing shoots, which tend to be very pithy). I remember getting some great citrus branches when a school replaced a Sarasota citrus grove. There's always pruning time, too, when lots of branches are on the ground.

Cedar: One of the few evergreen trees I've used. There's a bit of sap to contend with, but nothing like with fresh pine branches.

Myrtle: I think the kind I used was wax myrtle, but other varieties are worth trying, too.

Bottlebrush, Indian rosewood, viburnum: Several Florida woods that work well. One of my all-time favorite slingshot forks is viburnum—very, very strong and beautifully symmetrical.

Flowering crabapple, flowering plum: Ornamental trees that have good branches.

Apple, peach, quince, guava: Other fruit trees that have good branches with which to work.

Firewood

Hardwoods like birch, maple, and oak are perfect for making a bed of hot coals, which can be used to roast marshmallows or cook corn or potatoes wrapped in foil. If you have some wood left over after you finish all your whittling projects, you might want to celebrate with a fire and some good food.

Kitchen and Dining Room Projects

As I hope you will discover through this book, whittling is an enjoyable pastime you can do pretty much anywhere. It can be wonderfully relaxing and can take your mind off your troubles. But don't be fooled into thinking that just because whittling is simple and fun, the only things you can make are toys and games. You can make those things, as you will see in a later section, but you can also make useful things that are handy to have around the house.

Each of the projects in this section is an example of how whittling pieces can be useful and incorporated in to your home to serve a specific purpose. These projects work particularly well in the kitchen and dining room. Naturally, given the nature of the raw material used, these projects, when finished, probably won't make the cut for serving at a formal dinner at the White House for the first family of France, but they'll fit very well in a lot of other settings.

Some projects, like the Hors D'oeuvres Sticks and Stick Holders (page 22) and the Salt Dipper Spoons (page 25) can easily fit in a backpack to come along on your next camping trip. Then, you can have some of the comforts of home out on the trail!

Use these projects to add a personal touch to your kitchen or dining room. Some are perfect for gatherings with friends, and others can easily be personalized and given as gifts.

Hors D'oeuvres Sticks and Stick Holders

Here's a project that allows you to practice a foreign language and impress all your dinner guests. This is one of the quickest and easiest projects, but at the same time one that's fun to make and very practical. You're almost guaranteed to get a great reaction from the guests or company you're having over, especially if everyone at the event has his or her own personalized stick, complete with a custom-burned name on the handle end.

MATERIALS LIST

- Knife
- Variety of hardwood sticks
- Large branches to make the stick holders
- Drill and bits
- Handsaw or pull saw
- Pruning shears

Little Fact: *Hors d'oeuvres* is French. Translated literally, it means "outside of the work."

Find a group of thin twigs or branches that are relatively straight and of reasonably similar thickness. (Birch, maple, or some other hardwood is probably best.)

Cut the branches so they are more or less the same length. They don't have to be exactly the same, but it looks nice if they have a uniform appearance.

Slice the bark off one end of each stick. Leave enough clean wood to hold a marshmallow, a vegetable slice, or anything else you might be skewering. Taper and sharpen the point.

Round the opposite end of each stick, forming the handle.

Your finished sticks should look something like this. They don't need to match in size and thickness unless that's what you want. You can make sticks of different sizes to use with different foods.

You can make stick holders out of larger branches cut to resemble stumps or logs. You just need to drill holes for the sticks and make sure the bottom of the holder is flat and broad enough to stand upright while holding all the sticks.

6

Two Fondue Recipes for Your Campfire

Campfire Fondue

Ingredients:

1½ cups shredded cheddar cheese

2 tbsp. all-purpose flour

¼ tsp. paprika

1 can of Cheddar Cheese soup

½ cup beer, white wine, or water

Combine dry ingredients. Mix beer in with soup, then add dry ingredients. Heat over fire or on stove stirring in shredded cheese until melted. Serve with bread of choice.

Tip: For a more spicy fondue, replace the paprika with cayenne pepper

S'mores Fondue

Ingredients:

4 chocolate bars

2 cinnamon sticks

¼ tsp. paprika

¾ cup Kahlua

Graham cracker crumbs

Place all ingredients in a pan or pot and heat until chocolate is melted. Meanwhile, toast marshmallows or heat in the microwave. Dip marshmallows into chocolate mixture and enjoy. Marshmallows can also be placed between two graham crackers. Add strawberry slices to make a sweet treat even sweeter.

Salt Dipper Spoons

I can't remember the last time I saw a real little salt spoon with its accompanying miniature spoon, but I know they do exist. Maybe if we promise to use them wisely and not over-salt our food, we can get a new (old) salting movement going.

MATERIALS LIST

• Knife
• Forked branches
• Sandpaper
• Rotary tool

Wood vs. Plastic

Not only is a wooden spoon more natural than a plastic one, some studies suggest it is a cleaner utensil for your kitchen. Wood dries much more quickly than plastic, shortening the lifespan of bacteria on its surface. It is also naturally resistant to bacteria growth, which can help keep your kitchen free of germs.

? **Little Fact:** Hardwoods such as cherry, oak, and beech are best for making wooden spoons.

The "blank" for this project is a piece of wood that has a thin branch growing out of a larger branch. The thin branch will become the handle, and the short section of the larger branch will become the bowl of the spoon.

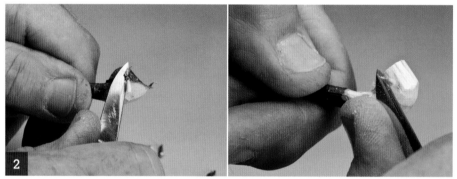

Remove the bark from the bowl branch and round it off to give it the basic shape you'd like it to have.

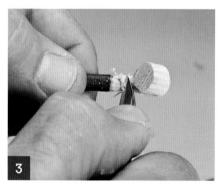

Take a little bark off the handle branch, blending the handle into the bowl piece.

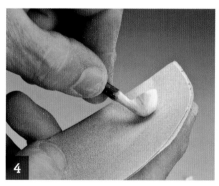

Sand the bowl smooth.

Little Tip: Keep wooden utensils looking like new by rubbing them with walnut oil.

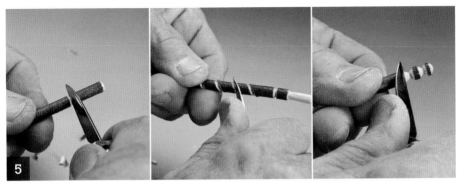

The dark bark contrasts beautifully with the light-colored wood underneath it. You can use a variety of notched or spiral cuts around the handle branch to decorate your spoon. There are all kinds of possibilities for carving the handle.

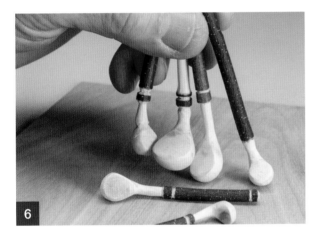

Of course you can vary the size of your spoons by choosing "blanks" of different sizes.

Hollow out the bowl with a rotary tool. If the bit is sharp, the bowl will match the color of the wood when you're finished. If the bit is dull, the bowl will have a burnt effect. With a dark bowl, you can see more easily how much salt you're picking up.

Stockade Toothpick Holder

This simple project can be scaled up or down to hold just about anything you can think of. It's good for office supplies like pencils, pens, and scissors, or it can hold your wooden spoons for cooking. Use it at a barbeque or picnic to hold silverware. Let your imagination run wild!

Flavored Toothpicks

Soak your toothpicks in flavored oils like those used for making candy. Eight hours or more will get you peppermint- or cinnamon-flavored toothpicks. Experiment with different flavors until you find your favorite.

MATERIALS LIST

- Knife
- Large branch at least 3" (75mm) in diameter
- Small straight branches or twigs
- Drill and bits
- Wood glue
- Rubber bands
- A small cylinder wrapped in wax paper (a thick marker will work)
- Pencil
- Pruning shears

Little Fact: Maine makes about 90 percent of the country's toothpicks.

Gather your materials and cut a slice from the large branch at least ½" (13mm) thick. For a taller toothpick holder, cut a thicker slice.

Draw a circle in the middle of the large slice, and then drill (or router) a ¼" (6mm)-deep furrow along the edge of the circle.

I drill holes around the circle's edge as close to each other as possible and finish the furrow by cutting away the remaining wood with my pocketknife.

Cut your thin branches into little stockade "logs" that will be glued into the circular furrow. If you want, round them a bit or bring them to a point to make them look like the stockade posts of an old frontier fort. Pointing them may help keep crawly critters from attacking your toothpick population.

Put wood glue in the furrow, place the wax-paper-covered cylinder in the center of the circle, and glue the little logs into place around it. Use a rubber band or two to help keep the sticks in place. This gluing can be a bit tricky, but you'll figure it out! Once the glue dries, remove the cylinder and fill up your holder with toothpicks.

MATERIALS LIST

- Dry seasoned wood
- Handsaw or Japanese pull saw
- Sandpaper
- Wood glue
- Magnets
- Colored permanent markers
- Woodburner

Magnets

This project will take you just minutes to finish. Cut slices of any seasoned dry wood and sand them smooth. Glue a good magnet on the back. Then, woodburn a design (or words) and color it in with permanent markers. If you make your slices from dry, seasoned branches, you won't end up with checking, splitting, or bark that peels off or loosens from the wood.

Some good woods for this project include holly, birch, maple, cherry, and basswood, but many others will work, too.

Magnet Compass

Make your own compass. Take a magnet and rub it over a needle, pin, or paper clip. Always rub the magnet in the same direction or it will not have any effect on your needle. Push the needle through a piece of cork or foam that is about ¼" (6mm) thick. Place the cork in a cup or bowl of water (make sure it is sitting on a flat surface). You now have a compass that will point to the magnetic pole closest to you.

Little Fact: You can find magnets in telephones, stereos, vacuums, and televisions.

Fences for Everything

Fences are great outside for keeping pesky animals away from your garden or for preventing your dog from visiting your neighbor's tree. Since they're so useful outside, why not make an indoor fence that's just as useful? These miniature fences can be scaled up or down as needed and have all kinds of useful and decorative applications. Use them as letter holders, napkin holders, or settings for whittled roosters. You can make personalized ones for your kids to hold school papers or homework. See what other uses you can come up with for this versatile project.

MATERIALS LIST

- Knife
- Scrap milled blocks for the base
- Branches for the fence *posts*
- Thin branches for fence *rails*
- Drill and bits
- Handsaw or Japanese pull saw
- Awl or nail
- Wood glue

Little Fact: Romans brought *mappae* (napkins) to dinner parties in order to carry home leftovers.

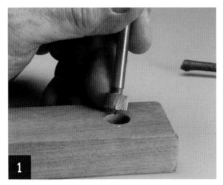

Make your base block, and use the drill to "dig" the holes for the fence posts. (I'm using a Forstner bit here.)

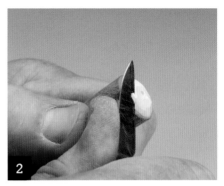

Take your knife and round the top of the branches you're using as your fence posts.

Use your saw and knife to narrow the bottom of each fencepost to match the diameter of the holes you drilled in the base block. Doing this allows the bottom of the fence post to overlap the hole slightly. It will probably look better this way than if you stick the post straight into the hole, especially if the fence post is not exactly round.

Backyard Fence

Is building a backyard fence on your to-do list? Consider building a split rail fence with cedar. Because of its simplicity, a split rail fence is easy to install—a great do-it-yourself project. It's also an inexpensive alternative to another fence style. Cedar wood is perfect for fence building because it is not affected by the elements as much as other woods.

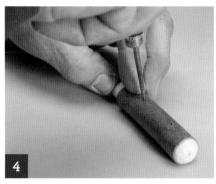

Using an awl (or nail), mark the locations on each fence post where you'll drill holes for the fence rails.

Drill the holes for the rails. (Drilling a dry, seasoned branch will produce a much cleaner hole than a green branch.)

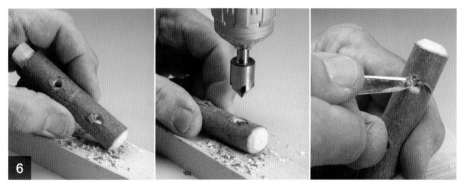

You'll probably end up with holes that are a little ragged, especially on the side of the post where the drill bit exits. Clean out the edges of the hole with a countersink bit, or clean off the rough edges with the tip of your pocketknife. If you use the pocketknife method, be careful to cut in a direction that allows you to keep as much bark as you want.

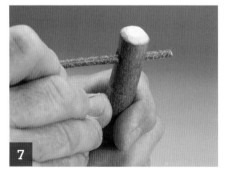

Insert the fenceposts into the base block and the rails into the posts, using a bit of wood glue to keep the fence tight.

Signed and Sealed

Letters were once closed with hot wax that was then stamped by the sender with a special symbol. The person who received the letter knew it had not been previously opened if this wax seal was still intact. Using the methods found throughout this book, try to whittle your own seal.

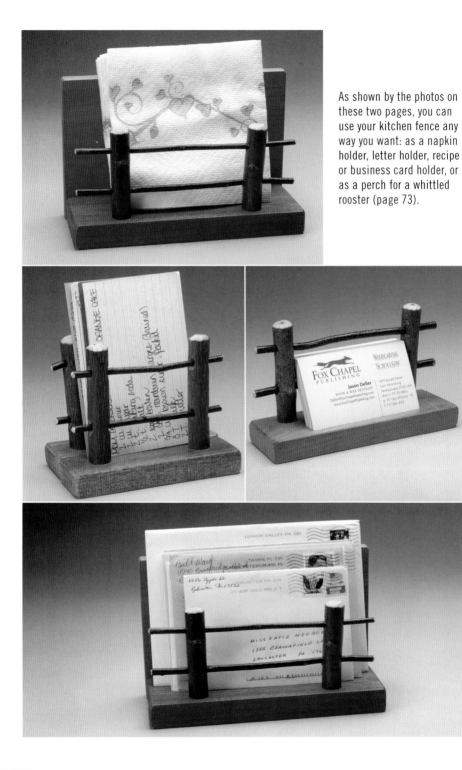

As shown by the photos on these two pages, you can use your kitchen fence any way you want: as a napkin holder, letter holder, recipe or business card holder, or as a perch for a whittled rooster (page 73).

The Language of Business Cards

Each country has its own traditions for accepting and receiving business cards. In China, Korea, and Japan, you should present your business card with both hands and always present your business card before you ask for another person's. In India and Islamic countries, you should always present your business card with your right hand. Remember not to cover up any important information when you're passing your card to someone else.

Home Decoration Projects and Gift Ideas

It's always nice when you can combine the decorative and the utilitarian. There are lots of things in this world that are immensely useful, but frankly don't look very attractive.

Then, there are things that are absolutely beautiful, but don't appear to serve any practical purpose. (Okay, okay, I'll grant that just being beautiful and having that beauty enjoyed can be considered useful, valuable, and practical.) In any case, the projects in this section, if not beautiful as such, are at least reasonably attractive *and* serve a useful purpose, even if that purpose is just to elicit a good laugh, like the Country Weather Station project.

Besides being practical and looking nice, every project in this section (and the whole book for that matter) makes a great gift. In the case of the knitting needles (page 53) and crochet hook (page 56), your gift recipient might even use your gift to make another gift for someone else. A project like the wreaths (page 38) can be decorated for any season.

Some of the finished pieces can be worn, others hung, and others set on a shelf next to a favorite photo. Still others might be used to make an heirloom table runner or a winter scarf. There are all kinds of opportunities here to put *your* creativity to work!

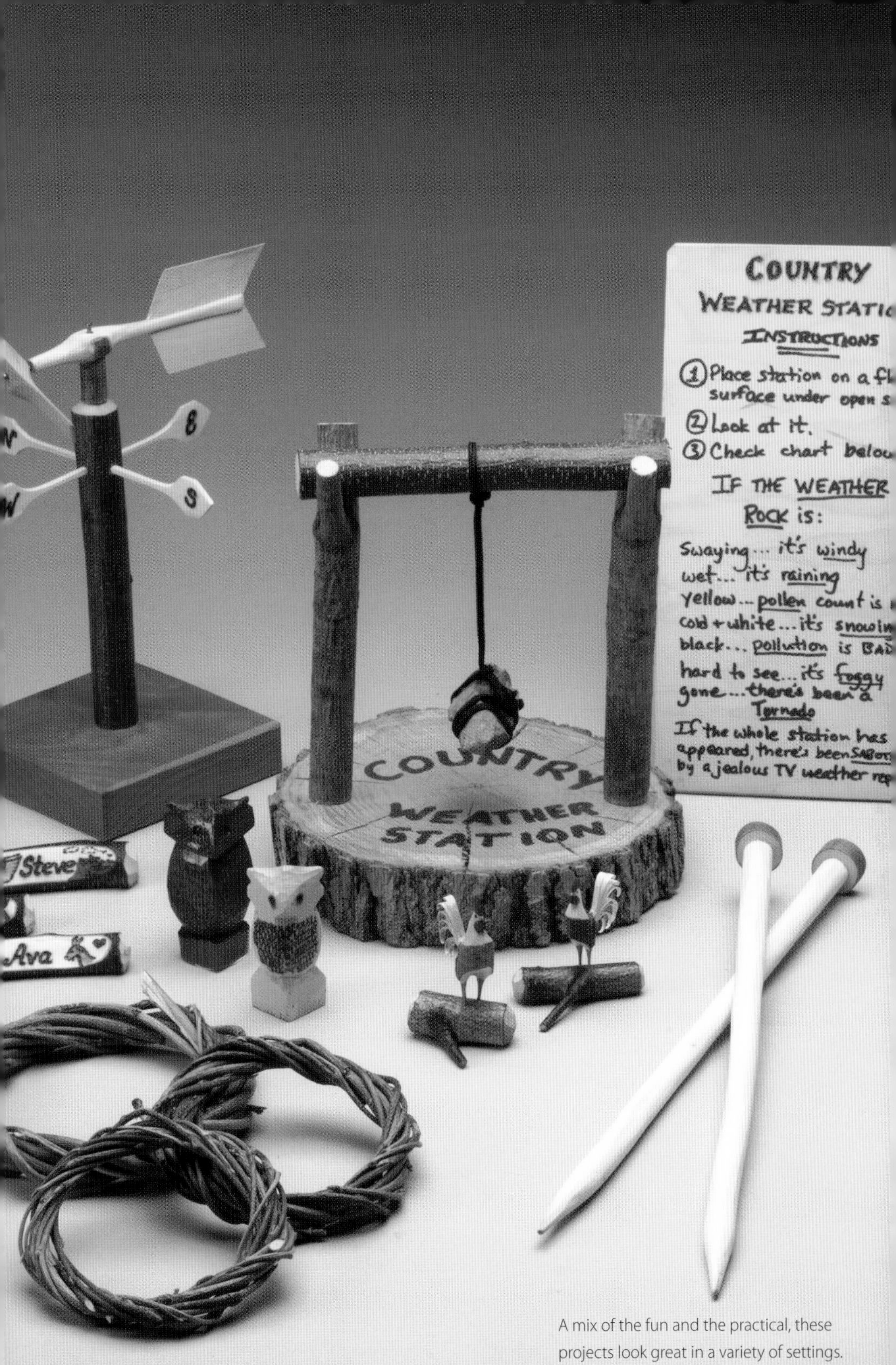

COUNTRY
WEATHER STATIO
INSTRUCTIONS
1 Place station on a fl
surface under open s
2 Look at it.
3 Check chart below

IF THE WEATHER
ROCK is:

Swaying... it's windy
wet... it's raining
yellow... pollen count is
cold + white... it's snowin
black... pollution is BAD
hard to see... it's foggy
gone... there's been a
Tornado
If the whole station has
appeared, there's been SABO
by a jealous TV weather rep

COUNTRY WEATHER STATION

Steve

Ava

A mix of the fun and the practical, these
projects look great in a variety of settings.

Wreaths

For the wreath shown here, I've used fresh weeping willow branches, although they don't necessarily have to be just freshly cut. If they've fallen naturally, but are still very flexible and not brittle, they'll work fine. Other long, thin branches work too, as well as various vines. Be careful not to harvest poison ivy though. It really is a beautiful plant, but I'm afraid the price you'll pay personally for using it may be a bit high!

MATERIALS LIST
- Weeping willow branches
- Knife for trimming branches

Little Fact: Cloth wreaths were worn to symbolize royalty in ancient times.

There are all kinds of application for wreaths. You can place almost anything in the middle—little carvings, photos, miniature trees, acorns, pine cones, sycamore balls, jingle bells—either gluing them in place or suspending them with thread, string, or ribbon. It's your project, your choice.

Of course if you make the initial circle much bigger and weave multiple branches or vines into the wreath, you'll end up with a much larger result. On the other hand, you can go much smaller with really tiny twigs and make ring-sized wreaths.

I started this project with a bunch of willow branches from my neighbor Fred's back yard. (Actually I think Fred would be glad if I took the whole massive tree. While it's a beauty much of the year, at other times it is super, super messy. Anyway, he was glad that I took some of the long, low-hanging branches.)

Notice all those tender spring leaves on the branches? They'll have to go. Run your fingers down each branch to get the leaves off.

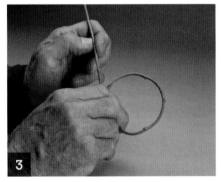

Form a circle with the thickest end of the branch.

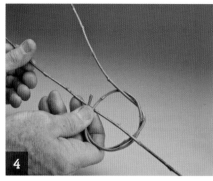

4

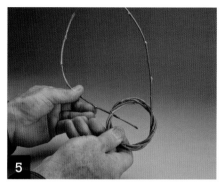

5

Keep wrapping the branch around the first circle you've made, weaving the point of the branch in and out of the circle.

The wreath will get thicker as you continue to weave the branch around the original circle, and eventually you'll come to the end of the branch.

6

Tuck the end of the branch tightly into the wreath. You may have to trim it if it sticks out too much. As the wreath dries it will harden and stay in the shape in which you left it.

Weeping Willow Facts

As its name implies, the weeping willow is associated with grief. In places like China and Turkey, planting the tree shows loss, usually of a loved one. The tree itself looks like it's crying when it rains. The water runs down the branches, dripping off the ends like tears. Despite these associations, weeping willows are vibrant plants that can grow seventy feet (21,336mm) high, and just as wide. Their root system is equally impressive, and homeowners should carefully consider where to plant such a tree, as it can damage basements, septic systems, and similar subterranean equipment.

COUNTRY
WEATHER STATION
INSTRUCTIONS

① Place station on a flat surface under open sky
② Look at it.
③ Check chart below.

IF THE WEATHER
ROCK is:

Swaying... it's windy
wet... it's raining
Yellow... pollen count is high
cold + white... it's snowing
black... pollution is BAD!
hard to see... it's foggy
gone... there's been a
    Tornado
If the whole station has disappeared, there's been SABOTAGE
by a jealous TV weather reporter.

Country Weather Station

This is a great project for any camper who needs a weather forecast while out on a trip, and it works great in your home, too. Put it on your porch or an exterior windowsill and check it before you leave the house and you'll always know how to dress. Actually, if you make one of these weather stations, you'll be able to tell the weather much more accurately than the average television weather reporter!

Depending on where you live, you might want to add an entry to the weather chart for conditions specific to your area.

MATERIALS LIST

- Knife
- Two Y-shaped branches
- One straight branch
- A slice of wood
- A small board
- String
- A small rock
- Drill and bits
- Handsaw or pull saw
- Permanent marker

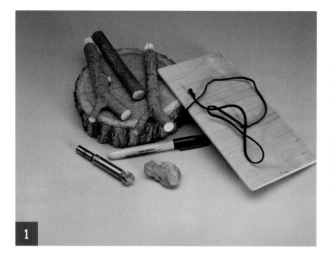

Gather your materials and tools and drill two holes in the wood slice. Taper the bottoms of the Y-shaped branches to fit the drilled holes. Write the name of your weather station on the wood slice with your permanent marker.

Here's what you should have after you've completed step 1.

Tie one end of the string securely to the rock and the other to the straight branch.

Insert the Y-shaped branches into the base and put the cross piece in place. Make sure the rock is able to swing freely. It must be so for total accuracy!

Country Weather Station

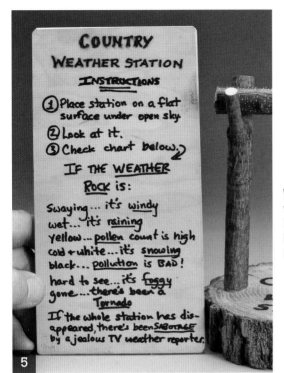

COUNTRY WEATHER STATION

INSTRUCTIONS

① Place station on a flat surface under open sky.

② Look at it.

③ Check chart below.

IF THE WEATHER ROCK is:

Swaying... it's windy

wet... it's raining

yellow... pollen count is high

cold + white... it's snowing

black... pollution is BAD!

hard to see... it's foggy

gone... there's been a Tornado

If the whole station has disappeared, there's been SABOTAGE by a jealous TV weather reporter.

5

With your marker, write out the weather station "Instruction and Interpretation Key" on the small board. Now you can marvel at your weather station's accuracy.

Weather Forecast

Can you predict the weather? Here are some tips to help determine what's coming your way.

1. Dandelions, tulips, and scarlet pimpernels all close up when bad weather is approaching.

2. Cows often lie down before it rains.

3. High white clouds indicate good weather, clouds forming a gray mist indicate rain, and low dark clouds grouped together indicate a storm.

4. Rising campfire smoke means good weather. Smoke moving sideways or dropping means bad weather is on the way.

5. Can't hear animal sounds around you? A bad storm is likely approaching.

6. Moisture saturates the air before a storm, strengthening the scents of plants around you, and making it smell like rain.

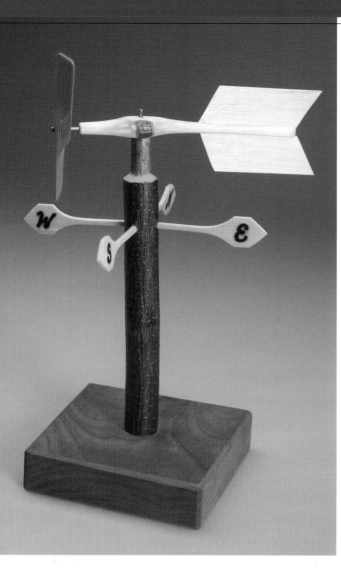

Weathervane

Pair this project with the Country Weather Station, and you'll be the best weather forecaster around. Don't be intimidated by the number of pieces needed to make the project. Just follow the steps and soon you'll be proudly assembling your very own weather vane. As with any project in this book, you can make your weather vane as large or as small as you want. As is usually my habit, I opted for very small.

MATERIALS LIST

* Knife
* Several straight "logs" (branches)
* Thin flat pieces of milled wood scraps
* Straight-grained wood for carving the propeller
* Block of wood for the base
* Sandpaper
* Small nails
* Screw
* Drill and bits
* Marker and pencil
* Wood glue
* Refill ink
* Woodburner (optional)

Little Fact: The largest weathervane is 48' (14,630mm) tall with a 26' (7,925mm)-long arrow.

1

Branches like this will serve as the main vertical stem of the weathervane. The one on the right already has the holes drilled for the North, South, East, and West direction indicator arms.

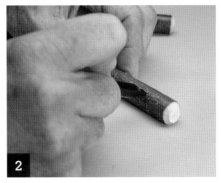

2

Mark the positions of the holes on the vertical stem that will hold your direction indicator arms.

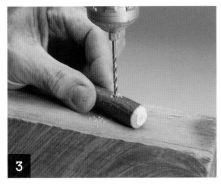

3

Drill the four holes.

4

Drill a hole in the top of the vertical stem, directly in the center. This will be used hold your weathervane arrow to the stem.

A Presidential Weathervane

In 1787, at the request of George Washington, a weathervane was built by Joseph Rakestraw and placed on top of the cupola of Mount Vernon. The weathervane was made in the shape of a peace dove, with an olive branch in its mouth.

Cut a little spacer log, smaller in diameter than your vertical stem, and drill a hole through its center. This will separate the stem and the arrow.

I used a blank like this one to carve the arrow shaft for my weathervane.

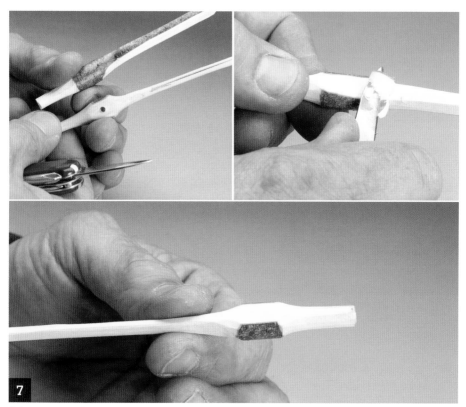

Select your own blank and carve the arrow shaft, leaving a wide, flat section about one-third of the way from the front of the shaft.

Drill a hole in the center of the wide, flat section of the arrow shaft.

Drill a hole in the center of the front of the arrow shaft. This is for the nail that attaches the propeller to the arrow. (If you try hammering the nail into the arrow without pre-drilling, you'll almost certainly split the shaft.)

Drilling Safety

For steps 8 and 9 of this project, I chose to hold the arrow shaft as I drilled it. If you are uncomfortable holding this piece while drilling, you can clamp it to your workbench instead. Using a clamp while drilling helps prevent workshop accidents.

I used a little bit of refill ink for a ballpoint pen to make a plastic bushing for the arrow by placing the refill in the pivot hole drilled in the wide section of the arrow shaft. The inside diameter of the refill was just a hair larger than the diameter of the nail I used to connect the arrow to the shaft.

With the tip of your knife, carefully carve a long groove on the top side and bottom side of the back half of the arrow shaft (behind the wide section). You will glue the fins here later.

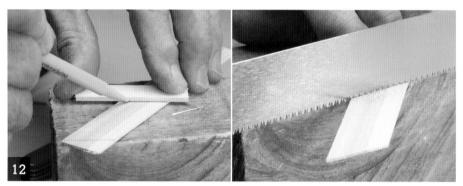

Take one of your thin wood scraps and cut out two little fins (make sure the wood is very thin). Sand them smooth.

Glue the two fins into the grooves in the arrow shaft.

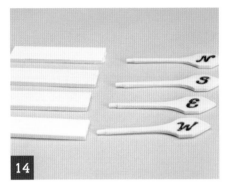

14

Carve the four direction indicator arms from four pieces of scrap wood. You can write or woodburn the letter for the directions on each arm. Make sure the ends of the arms will fit into the holes drilled at the top of the vertical weathervane stem and glue them into place.

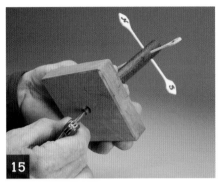

15

Screw the vertical stem onto a block base.

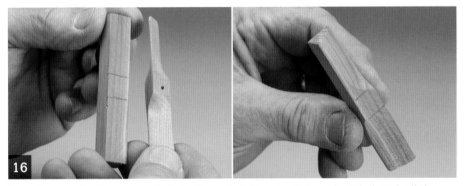

16

Carve the propeller. You can use just about any straight-grained piece of wood. (I used a little piece of cedar.)

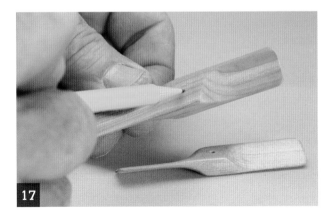

17

Mark and drill a hole in the center of the propeller. Make sure it's big enough so the propeller turns freely on the nail you'll use to attach it to the arrow. Nail the propeller to the arrow shaft.

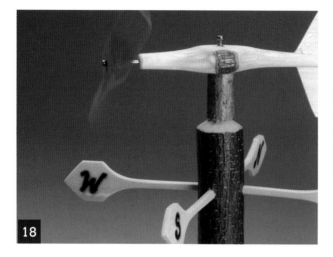

Attach the entire arrow and spacer log to the top of the weather vane's vertical stem using a nail. Now it's ready to sit outside and tell you which way the wind is blowing!

18

Wind Rose

The wind rose is a diagram used to show the wind patterns for a particular region. It can help meteorologists predict weather patterns by showing the directions from which the wind blows most frequently. A wind rose is set up as a series of lines radiating from a central point, like the spokes of a wheel. Each line points toward a specific direction, like North, or Southwest. The lines are drawn at different lengths. A long line indicates the wind often blows from that direction, while a short line indicates the wind infrequently blows from that direction. For example, a wind rose could have four lines, each pointing toward a cardinal direction (North, South, East, West). If the East line is twice as long as the West line, the wind comes from the East twice as often as it does from the West. Wind rose diagrams can also be color coded to show the speed at which the wind is moving and other similar factors.

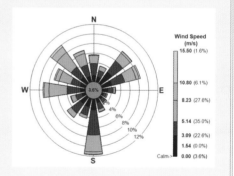

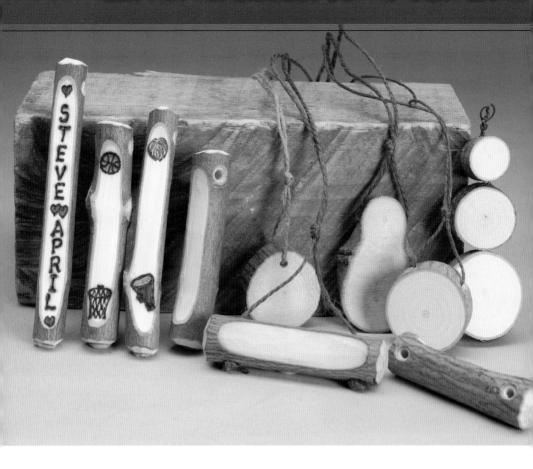

Pendants

Pendants are another great gift idea, easily
personalized to match the intended recipient's tastes
or interests. There are countless combinations
and design possibilities for pendants, and you can
use them to make necklaces, charm bracelets, or
anklets. You can make each pendant unique by
using branches and sticks of different sizes. Try long
thin branches for name pendants and branches with
a wide diameter for circular pendants that can be
decorated. Choose woods of different colors with
variation in grain pattern and bark texture. Finally,
you can always vary the angles you use to cut the
wood or the placement of the drilled holes to put a
spin on a pendant design.

MATERIALS LIST

- Knife
- Branches of varying sizes
- String or twine
- Sandpaper
- Handsaw or pull saw
- Drill and bits
- Colored permanent markers
  (optional)
- Woodburner (optional)

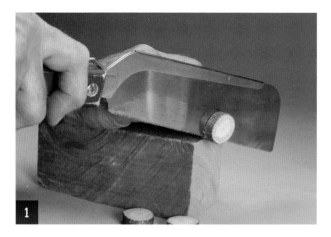

I've found that for cutting these small pieces, as well as larger ones, the Japanese pull saw is outstanding. The cuts are fast, clean, and, because of the thinness of the blade, very little wood is lost. All that is left to do after you cut out your pendants is drill holes in them for string, sand them if necessary, and decorate them with a woodburner and colored permanent markers.

With a variety of wooden beads, you can make all kinds of necklace patterns. Use whatever string you prefer. Pendants can be made in a great variety of shapes too. Notice, if you cut through a wood fork right where it branches apart, you get a piece shaped like a snowman.

Whittling Pendants

If you'd like to give yourself a challenge, try using the techniques in this book to whittle a pendant in the shape of your favorite animal, flower, instrument, or whatever you like. It's easy to personalize this project for yourself or a friend, and you'll be amazed by what you come up with.

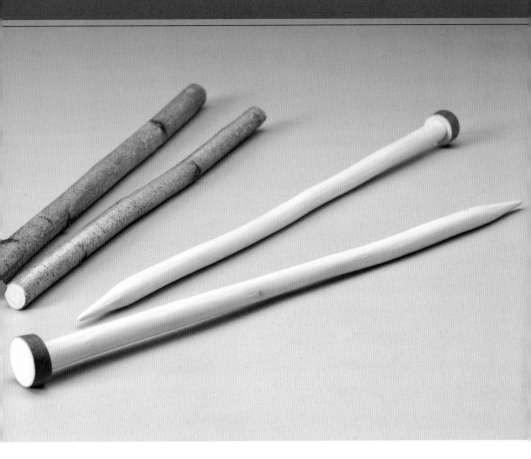

Knitting Needles

I personally have absolutely no experience with knitting, but I'm told that wooden knitting needles are warmer than metal ones, and quieter, too. Of course, they also work just as well. Whether or not they're actually better for people with arthritis, I honestly don't know, but I will say this: They're easy to make, and it's kind of fun to say, "I made these knitting needles for you, Grandma."

Who knows, perhaps once you finish this project, you'll be inspired to try your hand at knitting. I've heard that it's also a relaxing pastime, and when you're finished, you have a nice warm scarf or sweater to wear.

MATERIALS LIST

- Knife
- Long thin straight branches
- Thicker branches
- Sandpaper
- Wood glue
- Handsaw or pull saw

 Little Suggestion: Make fun needle toppers using clay that will harden in the oven.

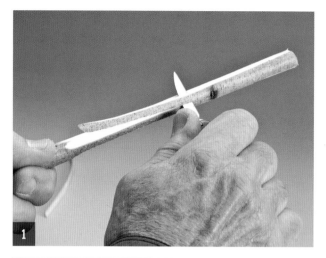

Start out with a couple of straight branches that are a bit thicker than the needles you want to make. (I'm sure if you don't have any straight branches handy you can always go for a commercially produced dowel, but somehow it seems using a branch would be more fun and a bit more natural.) Debark the branch, using long, straight strokes of your knife blade. Be sure not to take off too much wood as you slice away the bark.

Taper the end of each branch to a point. Not too sharp!

Sand the entire needle smooth. (If you're using a green branch, you'll need to wait until the piece dries a bit before you sand it, in order to get the smoothest result.)

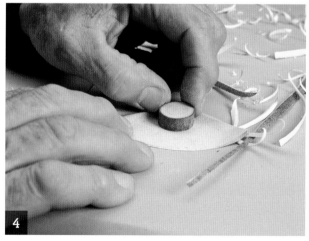

Cut a couple of small slices from a thick branch and sand the two sides smooth. Make them the diameter you want for the back ends of the needles.

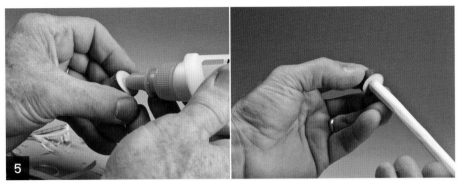

Using wood glue, attach the little slices to the end of each needle.

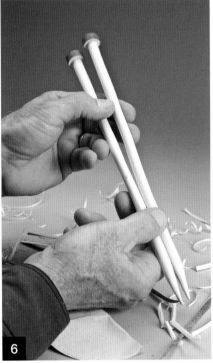

Ready to go. Now all you need is a few skeins of yarn, a pattern, and if you're in my shoes, someone who knows how to knit.

Keeping Warm

Here's some useful info about staying warm during cold nights in the woods (besides knitting yourself a nice thick sweater, that is!):

✓ Did you know that you lose over 75 percent of your body heat through your head? Wear a hat when you sleep to reduce this heat loss.

✓ When you make dinner, heat a pot of water and keep it by the fire until bedtime. Fill up some water bottles or other airtight containers with the water when you're ready to go to sleep and line your sleeping bag with them for an extra warm night.

✓ Keep out some of the chill from the ground by placing a plastic tarp or old shower curtain under the tent floor or your sleeping bag. It will also keep water from soaking into your sleeping bag.

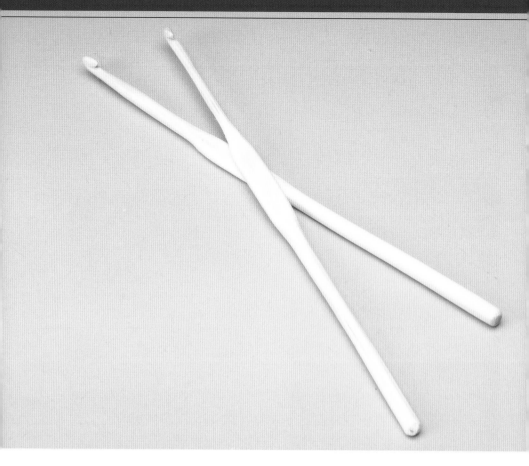

Crochet Hook

Crocheting is not quite the same as knitting, but the principal about a warmer tool still applies. Crochet hooks require a little more finesse with your knife to shape the hook and thumb rest. To help judge the shape you should be making, you might want to use a regular plastic or metal crochet hook as your pattern or model.

For those of you who do know how to crochet, or those who would like to give it a try, check out the pattern for making a simple crochet flower on page 58.

MATERIALS LIST

- Knife
- Long thin straight branch
- Sandpaper
- Pencil

Little Suggestion: Save your scraps of yarn and use them for a multi-color project.

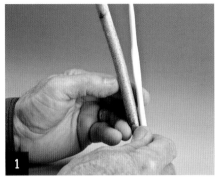

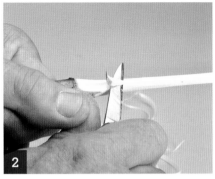

As with the knitting needles, the crochet hook calls for a straight branch, one that's thick enough to create the size hook for which you're aiming.

Taper the handle end of the branch, rounding it.

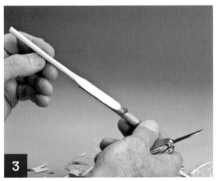

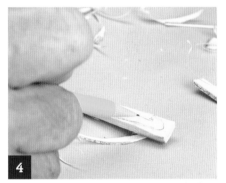

Flatten a section of the branch about two-thirds of the way from the bottom end of the hook. This is the thumb rest.

Now taper the other end of the branch, and, using a pencil, draw the outline of the hook itself.

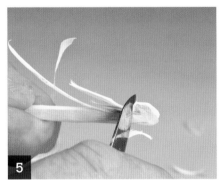

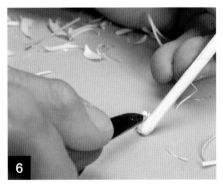

Very carefully cut out the hook. Make sure you go slowly as you cut toward the hook. You don't want to slice it off.

Using the tip of your blade, notch and shape the hook.

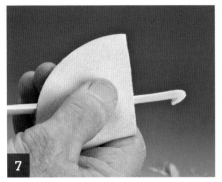
Sand the entire crochet hook smooth.

Now your crochet hook is ready to go to work!

Crochet Flower

A flower is a great accent to add to a hat or another piece of clothing, and crocheting one is easy. First form the center by chaining five stitches. Make a circle by connecting the first stitch to the fifth. Do ten double crochets and connect in the first double crochet. Make the petals by chaining two stitches, three double crochets in the next hook, chaining two stitches, and then connecting everything with a slip stitch. Repeat this four more times to create the remaining petals. You can add a special touch by gluing a sequin, seashell, or other decoration in the center of the flower.

MATERIALS LIST

- Knife
- Several branches of any thickness
- Sandpaper of medium to fine grit
- Handsaw or pull saw
- Woodburner
- Colored permanent markers (optional)

Name Logs

This project is the perfect time to use your woodburner to customize each log for yourself or for the person receiving it as a gift. I made the set shown in the photo above for a family I know quite well. Accompanying each name is a descriptive set of illustrations made to match each person's interests, occupations, or personalities. Obviously *your* names and drawings are going to be different, but just as meaningful and special.

Lincoln Logs

Lincoln Logs were introduced in 1916 by John Lloyd Wright, offering an alternative to basic children's building blocks. Wright credited the foundation of Tokyo's Imperial Hotel, an earthquake-proof structure designed by his father, Frank Lloyd Wright, with the concept for the logs. Lincoln Logs were promoted as educational toys, and were incredibly popular with the baby boomer generation.

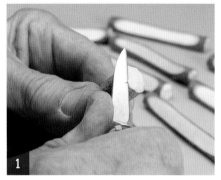

Cut a branch to the size you'd like for your log, and round both ends with your knife.

Cut out a swatch in the middle of the log. Make sure you cut from the each end of the log toward the middle, making these cuts meet. With a little practice you'll get the knack of matching up these cuts.

Flatten the bottom of the log so it doesn't roll away.

Sand the swatch you've carved on the front of the log. If you started with green wood, wait until the piece dries a bit before sanding it.

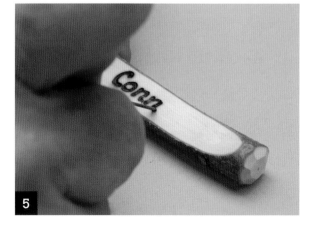

Woodburn the name and design(s) on the swatch. Color the drawings with permanent markers if you want the log to be a bit brighter. Natural shading with the woodburner also looks nice; it all depends on your taste.

BIG BOOK OF
WHITTLE FUN

Name Pins

Name pins are made in almost the same way as the name logs. You want to make sure your pins are not too large, though. Select branches that are about ⁵⁄₁₆–½" (10–15mm) in diameter and cut them into 2–3" (50–75mm)-long pieces. That way, your pins will always be just the right size. This is a great project to do with kids. You can put them in charge of decorating the pins as you carve more, or you can ask them to glue on the pin backs. They'll be thrilled when they get to wear and show off the finished product.

MATERIALS LIST

- Knife
- Several branches about ⁵⁄₁₆–½" (10–15mm) thick
- Heavy block or board
- Sandpaper
- Handsaw or pull saw
- Pin backs
- Wood glue
- Woodburner
- Colored permanent markers (optional)

Cut a branch into 2–3" (50–75mm)-long segments or logs. Take a log and round both ends with your knife.

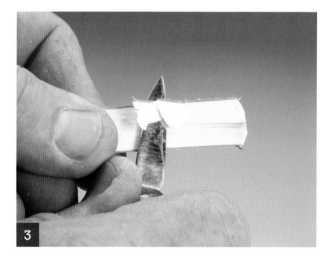

Split the log by placing it upright and positioning your knife across the center of the top. Use a board or heavy block to strike the knife and drive it into the log like an ax. One or two good hits should split the log in half.

Smooth the flat side of each half of the log with your knife.

Little Suggestion: Let your kids decorate their name pins to make them even more special.

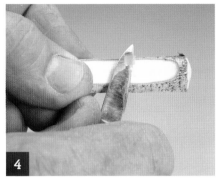

4

Flip the pieces over and cut a swatch on the round side of the pin, cutting from each end toward the middle.

5

Sand the swatch smooth.

Top Baby Names of 2011

Here are the top ten boys and girls names from last year.

Boys	Girls
1. Jacob	1. Isabella
2. Ethan	2. Emma
3. Jayden	3. Olivia
4. Alexander	4. Sophia
5. Michael	5. Ava
6. William	6. Addison
7. Joshua	7. Emily
8. Noah	8. Chloe
9. Daniel	9. Madison
10. Aiden	10. Abigail

6

Using carpenter's wood glue, glue a pin back on the flat side of your log.

Ax and Woodpile

The ax in this project is a perfect example of how you can use a forked branch to your advantage. Shaping the ax is much easier when you don't have to worry about trying to carve the entire piece out of a single straight branch. What you do with the finished project is up to you. It makes a great stand-alone decoration for your home or cabin, or you can pair it with a whittled critter, like a rooster. Perhaps you'd like to place it with the fences project from the previous section to give your countertop the look of a backyard scene.

MATERIALS LIST

- Knife
- Forked branch to make ax
- Thick branches to make logs
- Heavy branch to split logs
- Pencil
- Sandpaper
- Wood glue
- Paint (optional)
- Wood stain (optional)

Little Tip: Soak your ax handle in raw linseed oil if the head becomes loose.

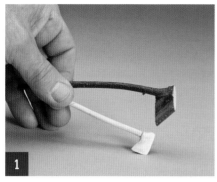

1

Find an ax "blank." A forked branch made of a thin branch connected to a thicker one is perfect. Here's an example next to an ax that's already been carved.

2

The thick branch will form your ax head. Start shaping the head by cutting off both sides of the thick branch.

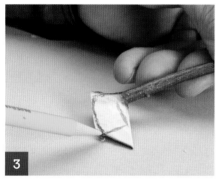

3

Sketch the profile of the ax head on the trimmed-down branch.

4

Carve the ax head and debark the handle.

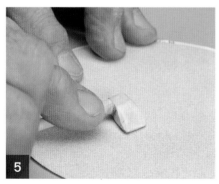

5

Sand the ax head and handle. If you want, you can stain your ax handle and paint the head.

6

Making a firewood pile simply consists of splitting a number of little logs.

?

Little Fact: A painted ax handle will give you blisters.

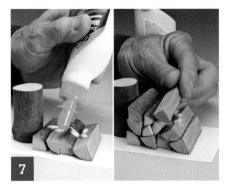

Glue the logs together in a pile.

Even though you did all the "log" chopping, your ax will sure look impressive sitting next to its very own woodpile.

Firewood

Finding dry wood to start a fire during or after a rainstorm can be simple if you look in the right places.

Fir and birch trees: Fir trees often have lower branches that have been cut off from the sun because of the growth of the upper branches. The lower branches die, making them perfect tinder for a fire. They are also often kept dry by the living upper branches. The bark of a birch tree contains a large amount of oil, which repels water, making it a perfect addition to your rainy day fire.

Fallen trees: Dead trees that have started to decay often contain dry wood. Look for these downed trees, strip off the bark, and use the inner wood for your fire.

Underneath: Look underneath large or fallen trees. You might find something that has been protected from the rain.

Branches: Wet branches are not an option for your fire, but you might be able to use the wood from dead branches if you strip off the wet bark.

Sap: The sap from pine trees can be used to help start your fire.

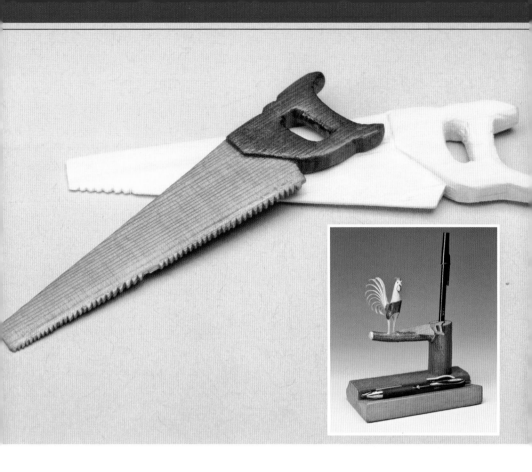

Saw

The miniature saw that follows (and any other tool for that matter) can fit into a number of settings. For instance, in a dollhouse workshop, or cutting into a stump that's part of a desk set. Here's the first piece I ever made that incorporated a saw. I think I finished this penholder sometime around 1980.

MATERIALS LIST

- Knife
- Straight-grained wood of choice
- Sandpaper
- Pencil
- Paint (optional)
- Wood stain (optional)

Little Tip: Use a wire saw to cut wood, plastic, bone, rubber, and some metals.

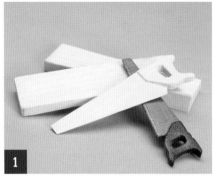

Select a straight-grained piece of wood from which to carve your saw (cedar, maple, poplar, and cherry are some good options).

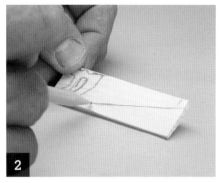

Draw the outline of the saw (both handle and blade) on the wood.

Cut away the wood around the outline of the blade to shape it. Make a cut at the back of the blade where the handle begins.

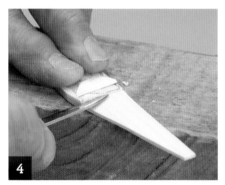

Thin the blade on both sides, forming the little step that constitutes the break between the handle and the saw blade.

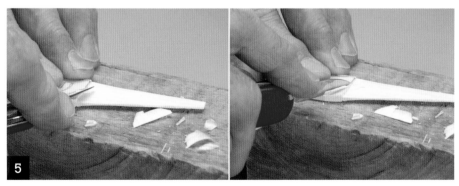

Shape the front angle of the lower part of the handle.

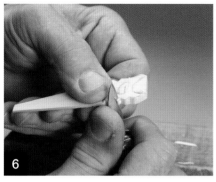

6 Shape the top and bottom of the front part of the handle.

7 Cut out the back of the handle.

8 With the tip of your blade, very carefully cut out the grip hole in the middle of the handle.

9 Sand both the blade and the handle smooth.

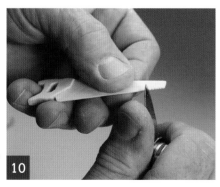

10 Cut teeth in the blade by making very, very tiny notches with your knife.

11 When your saw is finished, you can paint the handle and stain the blade if you want, as shown here.

Little Tip: Rub wax on your saw to help it cut more smoothly.

Miniature Knives and Letter Openers

While some of my previous books show how to make full-sized knives and letter openers, I thought it might be fun to show how a miniature version is carved. You can even cut them down to an action figure scale. Recently I've been carving the toothpicks I find next to restaurant cash registers.

If you need a sharp knife and are worried that the wooden version won't cut it, don't worry! Although a wooden knife can't do everything a steel knife can, it can certainly be sharpened and honed to complete most of the tasks for which you will need it. Remember, at one time steel knives weren't available, yet somehow our ancestors survived.

MATERIALS LIST

- Knife
- Straight, thin branches
- Pencil
- Sandpaper
- Colored permanent markers (optional)
- Woodburner (optional)

Little Fact: In Europe during the Middle Ages, knives, not forks, were the primary eating utensil.

For this project, you'll want a straight, thin piece of wood—like this piece of birch—but one that's not too small to carve.

Camping Must-Haves

Never leave on a camping trip without this essential gear: a phone, a flashlight, a watch, a whistle, **a knife**, a compass, and a first aid kit.

Round one end of the branch. This will form the back end of the handle.

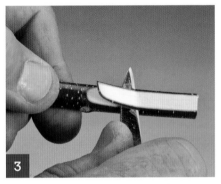

With long, straight cutting strokes, taper both sides of the blade portion of the branch.

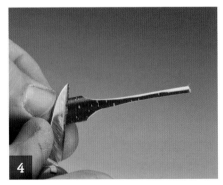

Make sure to cut an even amount from both sides.

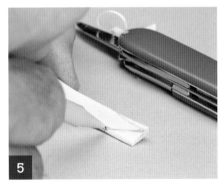

Draw the point of the blade at the end of the branch.

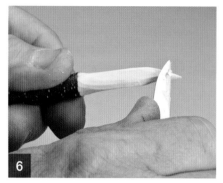

Shape the point of the blade.

Remove some wood where the handle and blade meet, clearly dividing the two sections of the knife.

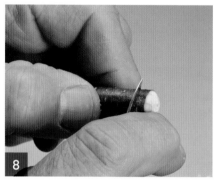

Cut a little notch around the back end of the handle.

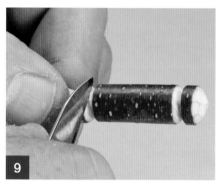

Cut another notch around the handle, this time closer to the blade.

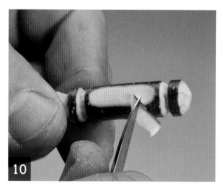

Cut out a little swatch on the handle. You can woodburn a name or design here if you'd like.

Sand the blade with fine sandpaper, making it as smooth as possible.

MATERIALS LIST

• Knife

• Forked branch

• Sandpaper

• Acrylic paint in red, yellow, and black (optional)

The Branch Rooster

For the forty-four years I've been whittling twigs and branches, the rooster has been my specialty—sort of the mascot of the whole branch-carving concept. It was the very first figure I remember seeing carved from a forked branch, and the first "critter" I remember doing myself. (Slingshot forks go back much further in my personal history, of course, but they don't count as "critters.")

My first Fox Chapel book, *Whittling Twigs and Branches,* has a detailed presentation of the branch rooster, showing roosters of many sizes and illustrating all the steps used to produce them. There's even a section in the second edition of the book that explains how to correct mistakes that can sometimes happen during the carving process.

I won't try to duplicate the whole rooster story here, but I would like to give you a complete enough description to make a small rooster to accompany any of the other little projects presented thus far. Here, I've basically reproduced a portion of my rooster-making instruction sheet, which has been distributed all over the world, both in English and Portuguese. Between the drawings, photos, and accompanying instructions, you should soon be able to whittle your own wood fork rooster.

Find yourself a forked piece of wood, where a thin branch joins a thicker one. If this is your first rooster, I suggest using a fork with a bottom branch (Branch B) that is about ⅜–¾" (10–20mm) thick.

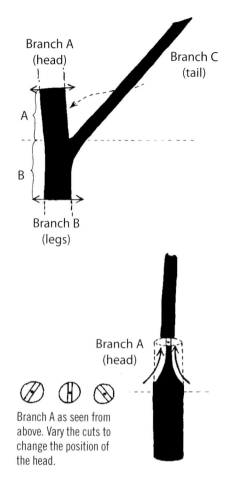

Branch A (head)

Branch C (tail)

A

B

Branch B (legs)

Branch A (head)

Branch A as seen from above. Vary the cuts to change the position of the head.

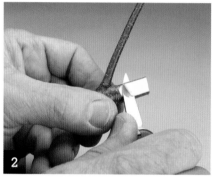

Taper Branch A to form the rooster's head and neck. Cut like this, with your thumb behind the wood.

Do not cut like this, with your thumb dangerously in line with the follow through of the knife blade.

BIG BOOK OF
WHITTLE FUN

The Branch Rooster

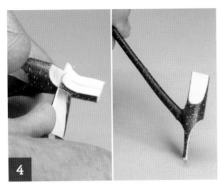

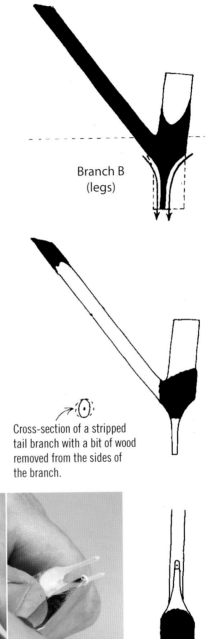

Branch B
(legs)

4

Taper Branch B to form the rooster's legs, taking more wood from the front than the back. This will give your rooster a puffed chest.

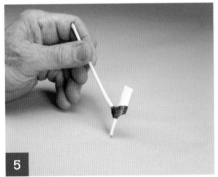

5

Remove the bark from all the branches, leaving only the rooster's "vest" of natural bark. For an all-white rooster, you can remove all the bark.

Cross-section of a stripped tail branch with a bit of wood removed from the sides of the branch.

6

Starting at the center of Branch B, cut two arches down and away from the body of the rooster to shape the legs (see diagram for the direction of the cuts). Don't cut toward the body of the rooster, or you will be cutting against the grain and risk cutting yourself.

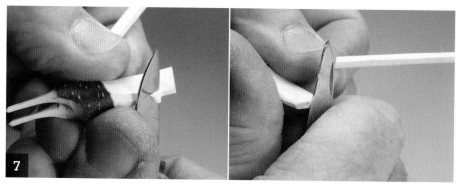

Shape the rooster's head by making three separate cuts. With the first cut, remove a small amount of wood from the front of Branch A. The second and third cuts are curved cuts at the top of the rooster. Make the angle of the backward curve (2) steeper than the frontward curve (3).

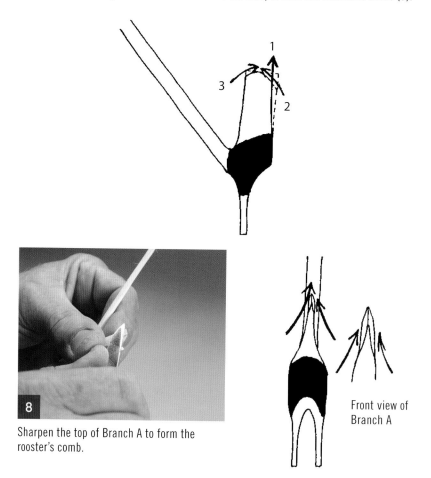

Sharpen the top of Branch A to form the rooster's comb.

Front view of Branch A

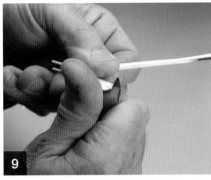

Notch the comb by making angled cuts that allow you to remove V-shaped pieces of wood from the top of the comb.

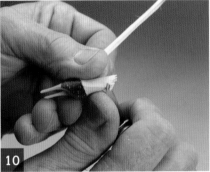

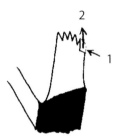

Make the two cuts shown in the diagram to form the front of the comb and the top of the beak.

Rooster Project Note

Especially on steps 10, 11, and 13 of this project, cut only a little at a time, making a 1 cut followed by a 2 cut, repeating these cuts as many times as necessary in order to get the desired shape. It's much better to make a number of shallow cuts than to dig in too deeply and end up splitting your project.

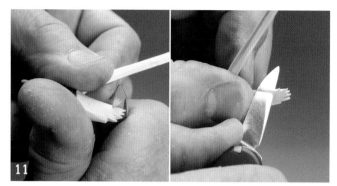

Make the two cuts shown in the diagram to form the back of the rooster's neck and comb.

Sharpen both the back of the comb and the beak.

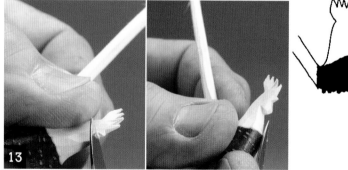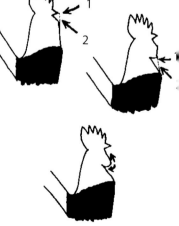

Shape the rooster's beak and carve the wattles. Round and smooth the wattles and the neck once you have the basic shape.

BIG BOOK OF
WHITTLE FUN

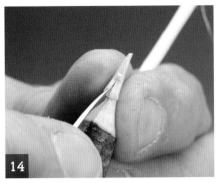

14 Split the wattles by making a thin V-cut with the tip of your knife blade.

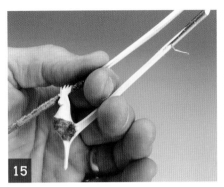

15 Now we're ready to do the tail, the step in the process that seems to give most people a bit of grief. Before attacking the tail branch of the rooster you're carving, you might want to practice on a scrap branch that is the same size as the rooster's tail branch.

Secure the end of the branch by tying it to a non-slip surface. Use short, repeated, forward-slicing motions, to produce thin strips of wood. Make the strips as thin as possible without actually slicing them off.

16

Camping Pets

You should think long and hard about bringing a real live pet (and not just your whittled rooster) on a camping trip. Taking your pet on a trip could expose it to diseases it would not encounter at home. In the woods, your pet might also encounter poisonous plants, animals, or reptiles. Bears and other predators are also a risk factor to consider if you're thinking about bringing your pet.

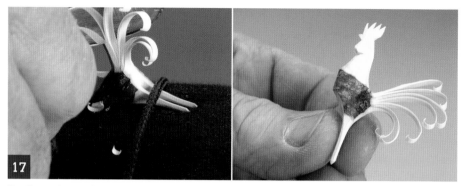

17

Now that you've practiced, use the same method on the rooster itself. (You'll note that I've tied the rooster to my knee to keep it still while I work.) Remember, use short, repeated, forward-slicing motions. Make sure you take the cuts all the way down to the base of the tail branch.

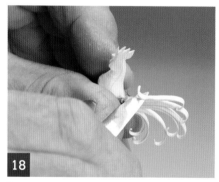

18

When you've made the last feather (the top one), thin it a little, cutting from the bottom up.

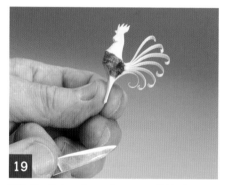

19

With the flat surface of your small blade, spread the feathers apart into the position in which you want them to stay.

20

Finish your rooster by carefully sanding its head and legs. Paint the rooster with red, yellow, and black acrylic paint if you want, painting the comb and wattles red, the beak and legs yellow, and using black for the eyes.

Branch Owl

Back in the summer of 2009, D. K. Klug of Mobile, Alabama, very kindly sent me one of his little owls, carved from a small block of wood. Accompanying it were some sketches and hand-written instructions. Mr. Klug was also generous enough to give me permission to share his ideas with anyone who might be interested. So, for this project, I've taken the basic idea of the little block owl and transfered it to a round branch. Of course it comes out a bit different, but the principle is the same. Mr. Klug's owl is the dark one at the right side of the photo above.

MATERIALS LIST

- Knife
- Straight branch of desired thickness
- Pencil
- Woodburner (optional)

1

Select a straight branch and cut off a blank. The thickness and length of the blank will determine the final size of your owl. This one is about the size of my thumb.

2

Make four notches around the branch a little less than one-third of the way from one end.

3

Do the same on the opposite end.

4

Make cuts to taper the wood up toward the head and down toward the base. Only do this about three-quarters of the way around the branch.

Visual Aid

Owls are known for their ability to turn their heads "backward." This is because an owl's eyes cannot move within their eye sockets, so they have to be able to turn their heads in all directions in order to see.

Bad Luck?

Throughout history, a hooting owl has been thought to signify bad luck. An owl usually hoots as a way of marking his territory. If you hear an owl hoot at night, it is probably because you have wandered into an area that he considers his own.

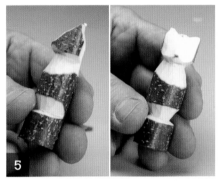

5 Shape the owl's head, being especially careful with the ears. (Mr. Klug said he's had to make penguins out of owls that have had their "ears" chopped off!)

6 Debark the bottom back of the branch and mark the owl's tail feathers.

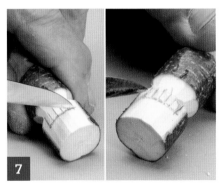

7 Using the tip of your blade, make little grooves on the lines you've drawn.

8 While D. K.. Klug uses a couple of different little tools to do the eyes and breast feathers on his block owl, I just use my woodburner's writing tip. I'm sure there are many ways to get the desired effect.

Sports, Games, and Leisure Projects

Ever since I was a little kid, I remember enjoying sports and games of all kinds. As I've heard the story told many times, my New York City-born dad (who as a boy attended baseball games during the Babe Ruth and Lou Gehrig era) gave his little Brazilian-born son (me) a baseball. Imagine his distress when I *kicked* it! Seriously, what did he expect? After all, I was born in a world-class soccer country.

To his delight, I'm sure, I did end up being a half-decent baseball player, though my strongest sport continued to be soccer. Then there was basketball, track, canoeing, volleyball, table tennis, swimming, marbles, tops, bottle caps (yes, on the dirt streets of Contamana, Peru, bottle caps was a popular game), and even occasional games of golf and bowling. I don't suppose tree climbing and tree house building are sports, but I did have all kinds of fun with them as well. Oh, and I forgot about slingshot hunting and pigeon and armadillo trapping.

Pretty much all of the sports I've played in my sixty-seven years have been on a normal scale in size. However, since my whittling/carving experience has led me mostly into miniature-scale productions, the majority of the sports and games projects that follow are on a very small scale.

These miniature projects are the perfect way to take your favorite sports game or other pastime with you everywhere you go.

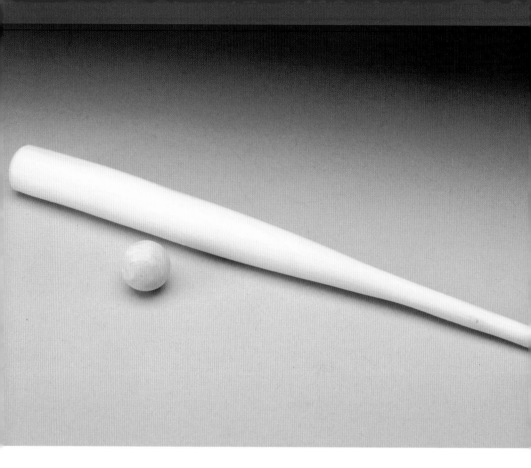

Baseball

If you want to make a cool frame for a baseball picture, you can buy a plain wood frame and glue the bat, ball, and home plate onto it, or you can put together a couple of teams made of action figures and have them play ball! You might have to enlist a bit of help from Hasbro, Mattel, and Bill Gates for this latter suggestion, though.

Pay attention to the technique used on page 89 to carve the baseball. You'll see the same or similar process used to carve a football and a golf ball in later projects, so get some practice in now.

MATERIALS LIST

- Knife
- Straight-grained pieces of wood
- Flat piece of milled wood
- Sandpaper
- Pencil
- Ruler
- White paint (optional)

Little Fact: The first professional baseball league was started in 1871.

You'll need to use a straight-grained piece of wood for this project, like a knotless branch or a straight-grained scrap of milled lumber.

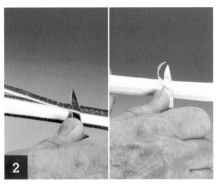

Using long, straight cutting strokes, remove the bark from the branch. The branch I'm using here is about ½" (15mm) in diameter.

Round the top end of the bat.

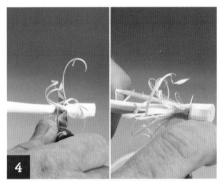

Taper the handle of the bat. Be sure to leave enough thickness at the end for the knob.

Road Trip Game

The car ride to your next sports event or favorite camping location might be a long one. Try playing this game to help the miles fly by: Pick a category like cities, states, countries, animals, etc. Have one person start by naming something from that category. The next person also names something from the category, but he must name something that starts with the last letter of the previous word. For example, if the category is cities and the first person names Paris, the last letter is an *s*. The next person must name a city that starts with *s*, like Savannah. Now the next person must name a city that starts with an *h*, like Heidelberg, and so on.

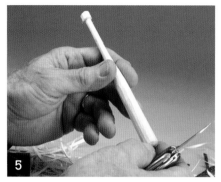

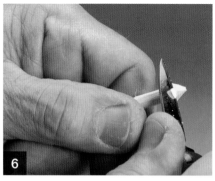

You'll end up with something like this.

Trim the knob so it matches the proportions of the rest of the bat.

Sand the whole bat smooth.

Select another straight-grained stick to carve the baseball. Remove the bark from one end of the stick.

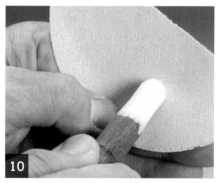

Round the end of the stick, making it as circular as possible.

Sand the end of the stick to make it as smooth and round as possible.

Little Fact: In the 1850s, baseball players often made their own bats.

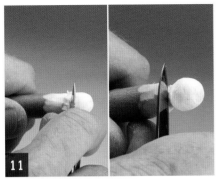

11

Using your knife, cut out the other half of the sphere.

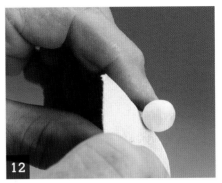

12

While the ball is still attached to the stick, sand what you can of the bottom of the ball.

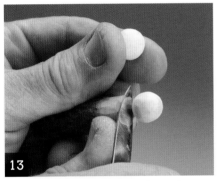

13

Remove the ball from the stick by cutting away the remaining wood between the two pieces. Finish smoothing the ball with a bit of sandpaper.

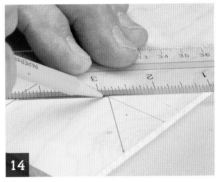

14

Using a little flat piece of milled wood, draw home plate to scale and cut it out. Sand it and paint it white.

How to Throw a Curve Ball

The curve ball is a throw that gives the pitcher a lot of control, because he can keep a solid grip on the ball. Topspin is the most important factor for this pitch. If a pitcher does not put enough topspin on his throw, the ball will not curve.

The grip:

Find the place on the ball where the seams are widest apart. Put your middle and index finger on one of the seams. Hold the ball tightly with your thumb, index, and third finger with your ring finger and pinky tucked back against your palm. Do not let the ball touch your palm, however. Now you are ready to throw.

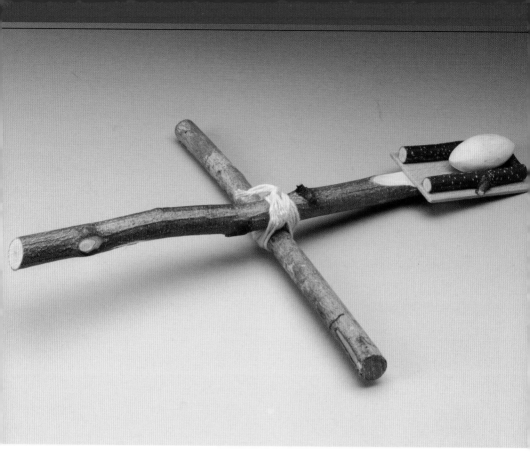

Football

Granted, this football is of the itsy bitsy size, but I bet Aaron Rodgers and Peyton Manning might get a charge out of it. True, they're quarterbacks and not kickers, but who knows, maybe once or twice they fantasized about kicking a game-winning field goal. At least I'm sure there have been numerous occasions when they were more than happy when their respective kickers won a game for them.

MATERIALS LIST

- Knife
- Thick straight branch for football
- Three 16" (410mm) or so sticks for goal posts
- Two 10" (255mm) or so sticks for launcher
- Launcher pad of choice
- Two forked sticks
- Launcher mounting base (optional)
- Wood glue
- String
- Sandpaper

Little Fact: Football, rugby, and soccer probably evolved from the Greek game harpastum.

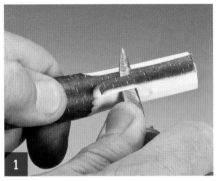

Select a thick straight branch to use as your blank. Remove the bark from one end.

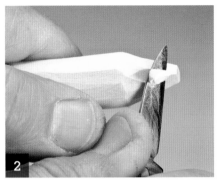

Taper and shape the end of the branch to form one point of the football.

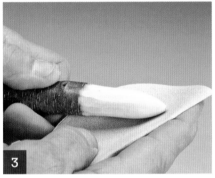

Use sandpaper to finish shaping and smoothing the carved end of the football.

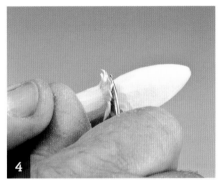

Carving backward from the middle of the ball, begin shaping the other end of the football.

Get a Grip

The key to a good throw with a football is the proper grip. Keep your thumb and middle finger just under the white ring at the end of the football. (Your fingers should be on the side of the ring that is closest to the center of the ball.) Put your other fingers on the seams and rest your index finger near the point of the ball.

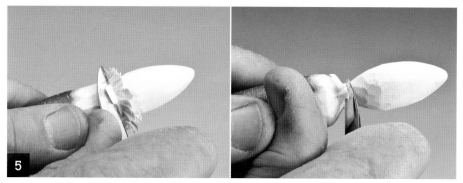

Keep notching out and tapering the unfinished end.

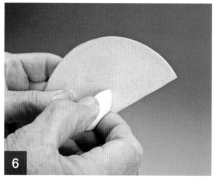

Cut the ball from the stick. Sand and smooth the newly carved half, blending it into the first half. Do any final cutting and sanding to get the ball to the shape of a regulation football.

Now that you have finished your football, you need something to send it flying through the air. See the instructions in the box below for making your very own miniature football launcher.

Building a Launcher

Glue two small branches to a flat piece of wood, and glue the entire piece to the end of a long stick. Tie the stick to a shorter crosspiece. Take two forked sticks and screw them into a block base (or stick them in the ground if playing outdoors). Place the crosspiece of your launcher across the forked sticks. Set your football in the launch holder and give the other end a whack to send the ball sailing. You can choose to make your launch holder out of other materials, too, like bottle caps, small jar lids, or half a walnut or pecan shell. Make a goal post for your launcher by tying a crossbar to two vertical branches or dowels.

Little Fact: Walter Camp is known as the "Father of American Football."

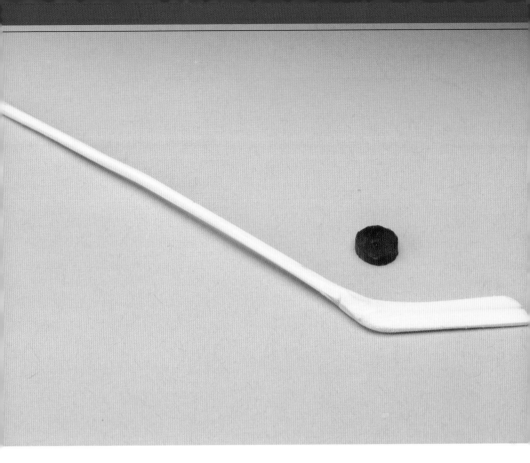

Ice Hockey

Having spent a good part of my childhood in the tropical parts of Brazil and Peru, about the only ice I ever saw was in the little freezer section of our kerosene refrigerator. Come to think of it, I do remember a couple of times when during a cold snap, the water on top of a bucket behind our house in Aquidauana, Mato Grosso, got a little crust of ice. I'm fairly sure I didn't even know a game like ice hockey existed until later on in life when we came to "Grandma's Land." Actually, would you believe that my mom wouldn't even let my brother and me go swimming in our neighbor's pond if the temperature dipped below 80 degrees? Too cold! But, I digress. Let's get to ice hockey.

MATERIALS LIST

- Knife
- Forked branch for stick
- Small slice from branch for puck
- Sandpaper
- Black permanent marker
- Black paint (optional)

Little Fact: In 1877, the *Montreal Gazette* printed the first known set of hockey rules.

1

Select a blank for your hockey stick. Look for a forked piece of wood that has a straight branch jutting out from the thicker branch.

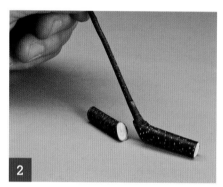

2

Trim the branch so it forms an L-shape, like a hockey stick.

Campfire Pizza

The next time you're out on a winter camping trip, try this pizza recipe by the fire to warm up. Or, make it at home after your child's hockey game.

Ingredients:

Loaf of bread

Jar of pizza sauce

Shredded cheese

Pepperoni or other pizza toppings (already cooked)

Butter

Pie Iron

Directions:

Heat pie iron over campfire. When hot, open and butter both sides. Place a slice of bread on each side. On one side place pizza sauce, pepperoni and cheese. Close iron, making sure other side is on top. Hold over fire, flipping every few minutes to make sure each side is toasted.

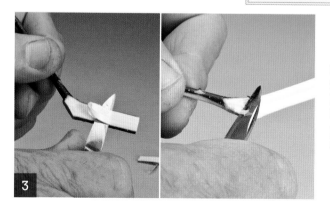

3

Flatten both sides of the thicker branch, carefully blending it into the handle. Remove the bark during this process. This will be the blade of the stick.

BIG BOOK OF
WHITTLE FUN

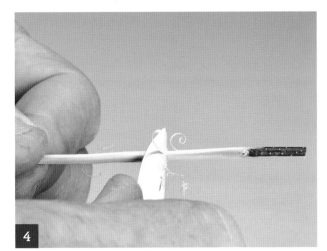

Using long, straight cutting strokes, remove the bark from the handle branch.

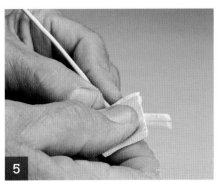

Sand the whole stick smooth.

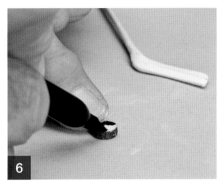

To make a puck, cut a slice of wood from a branch, sand it, and paint or color it black.

Ice Fishing

If you go ice fishing on your next camping trip, use a 4–5" (102–127mm) auger to cut your hole in the ice. Using a hammer and chisel or a power auger can create too much noise and scare your fish away.

Little Tip: Make a hockey puck by baking a potato in coals for three hours.

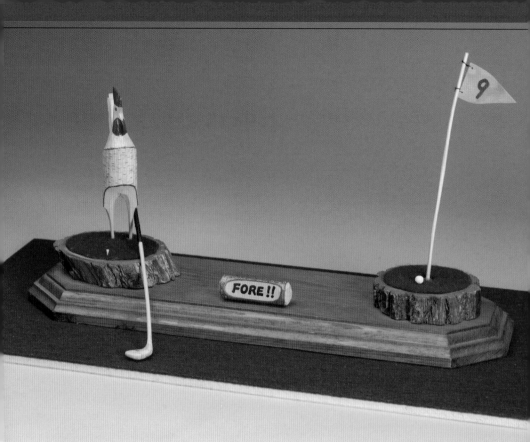

Golf

Golf is another sport with which I haven't had much experience. I have maybe played a total of ten games in my entire life. I live for the three or four great (lucky?) shots I make in an eighteen-hole round. It is fun to carve out little golf clubs, though. As you can tell from the photo, I've even carved a golf-playing rooster. He made a spectacular hole-in-one with a number four iron—off a tee! So you can see the ball, I've retrieved it from its hole-in-one position and placed it just outside the hole, ready to go in.

MATERIALS LIST

- Knife
- Forked branch for club
- Thin branch for golf ball
- Very thin twig for tee
- Thin twig for flagpole
- Flat piece of milled scrap wood for flag
- String
- Sandpaper
- Drill and bits
- Handsaw or pull saw

Little Tip: A regulation golf ball contains 336 dimples.

Select a blank for your golf club. Like the hockey stick project, you're looking for a forked piece of wood with a thin branch connected to a thicker one.

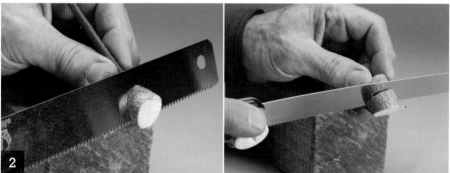

Saw off the top half of the thicker (club head) branch.

Here's what you'll have left—you can see the makings of a golf club already; you just have to do some shaping.

Shape the head of the golf club with your knife. (You can use an actual golf club as your model.) Then, sand the head smooth with a bit of sandpaper.

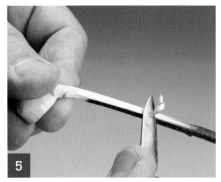

Remove the bark from the handle of your golf club.

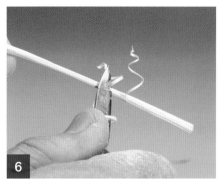

Taper the shaft so it is thinner toward the head of the club and thicker toward the grip. This tapering can be a little tricky, because the branch itself will have a natural shape that is the complete opposite—thicker toward the head and thinner toward the grip.

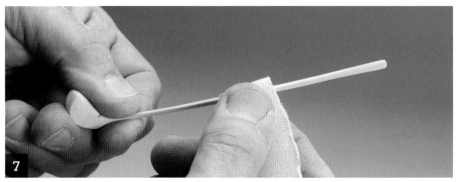

Sand the entire club smooth.

Outlawed

A law in Scotland decreed that men had to practice archery every day so they would be prepared in case the country was invaded. In the fifteenth century, however, many men were found playing golf instead of practicing their marksmanship, so King James II outlawed the game to try to force the men back to their duties.

Little Fact: Scotland's Musselburgh Golf Club hosted the first women's golf tournament in 1811.

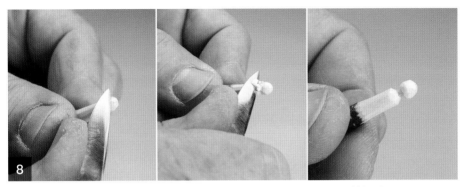

Carving a golf ball is basically the same as carving the baseball (see page 89) only on a smaller scale.

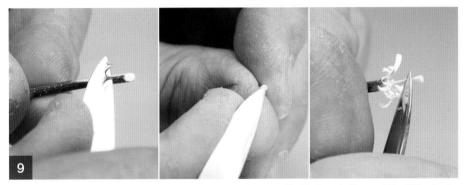

Carve a golf tee out of a very thin twig. Use the tip of your knife blade to hollow out the little dip in the top of the tee to hold the ball.

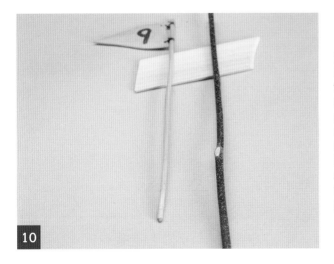

Making the flag is pretty logical. Make the pole from a thin twig. Remove the bark, straighten, and sand it. Cut a flag from a thin piece of scrap wood. Drill two very small holes in it, and tie it to your flagpole using string. Now all that's left is to set up your own "mini" golf course.

SILVER BAY PUBLIC LIBRA

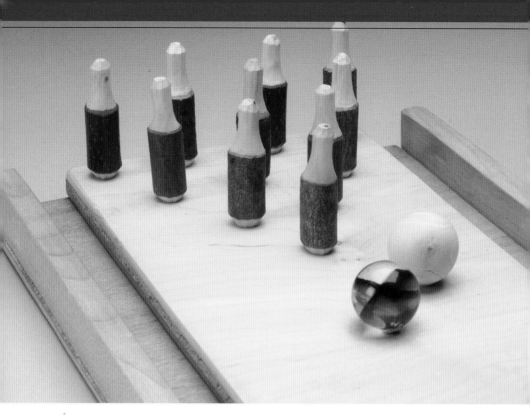

Bowling

As an athlete, I consider myself a sort of jack-of-all-trades and master-of-none, but bowling, well, that's where I've had some of my poorest experiences. When I first started dating my wife in college, even she beat me. As much as I love and admire Sheri for her many wonderful abilities and qualities, even she will admit that she's not exactly athletic and coordinated, and after more than forty-four years of a very good marriage, she still holds her bowling victories over me!

You'll start this project by making the bowling pins. While you don't really need a formal lane, I'll go ahead and show you how to make one of those too, complete with scratch line and gutters (after all, what's bowling without gutter balls?). The lane has been tested, and it works. However, I'd almost be willing to bet there won't be very many 300 games on it.

MATERIALS LIST

- Knife
- Several straight branches
- Bowling ball of choice
- Plywood and/or milled wood strips
- Handsaw or pull saw
- Hammer and nails
- Wood glue
- Paint or colored permanent markers

Cut ten equal-sized pieces from straight branches to serve as your pin blanks. The size of each piece will determine the size and scale of the pins. The size of my pins was more or less determined by the size of the lane I built—which in turn was determined by the size of the scrap pieces of wood I had on hand.

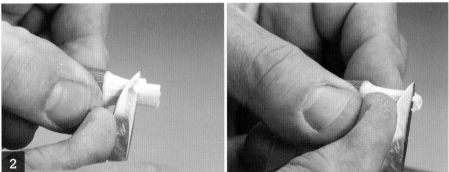

Taper the top of the each pin, removing the bark. Then, round the very top.

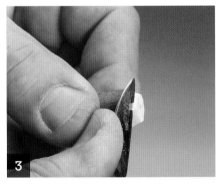

Round the edge of the base of each pin slightly, making sure the bottom remains flat so the pin stands steady and straight.

Here we have ten bowling pins and some bowling balls. You can use a large marble as the bowling ball or a ready made wooden ball, available at a craft supply stores. You can also make your own bowling ball using the method for making a baseball (page 89).

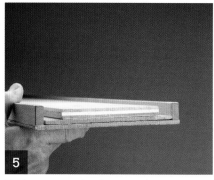

5 Making your own bowling lane is easy. Take whatever plywood boards and milled wood strips you have available and glue and nail them together.

6 At the pin end of the lane, mark where each pin should be placed with a dab of paint of a permanent marker.

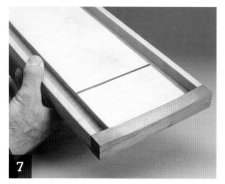

7 At the bowler's end, paint or draw a scratch line. I also finished my lane with an end piece that is tapered down to the surface level of the lane itself.

8 You can give your bowling lane an extra touch by building a little box to catch the pins that get knocked down. Make the interior walls of the box a hair wider than the outside walls of the lane, so you can easily slide it into place. Then it's time to start the game!

How Many?

Most bowling balls have three holes, but what is the highest number of holes your bowling ball can have? You may have a hole for each finger and thumb along with vent holes for each of them. You are also allowed a weight hole (used to help balance the ball) and a mill hole (used for inspection). That's twelve total!

BIG BOOK OF
WHITTLE FUN

Rowboat

I'm definitely not a musician, but I have learned to pick out quite a few tunes on my Hohner Echo 48-hole harmonica (by the way, a very forgiving instrument and a good one to learn on if you're even half-interested). I have even occasionally whittled and played at the same time, making use of one of those hands-free harmonica holders.

Over the years, my grandchildren have no doubt been the biggest fans of my limited musical abilities and bedtime harmonica concerts. While two-year-old Kennedy's current favorite is the ABC song, a short while back it was "Row, Row, Row Your Boat." I haven't shown Kennedy my little rowboat project yet, but when I do, I bet she'll go back to requesting the accompanying song, and it will be back at number one on the chart.

MATERIALS LIST
- Knife
- Block of wood for the boat
- Thin straight-grained wood scraps for the oars and seats
- Dry dock
- Pencil
- Small chisel
- Sandpaper
- Wood glue
- Rubber band

Little Fact: The best oars are made from spruce or ash.

I carve my little rowboats using dry docks, which are simply pieces of wood nailed to my workbench to hold the project in place while I work.

While a lot of the carving for this little boat is done using a freehand method—that is, holding the block of wood in one hand, with the knife in the other—there are some steps during which it is much more practical, and safer, to use a "dry dock," like the one shown above, to hold the boat. (I'm sure you could use some kind of vise, too, as long as it doesn't squeeze the wood too hard and dent it.)

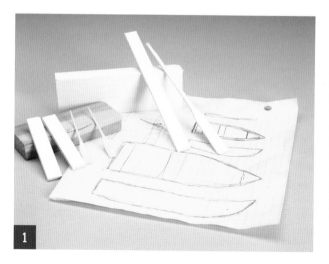

Gather your raw materials and make sure they are scaled to size. If you start out with a large block for your rowboat, you will want large pieces of scrap wood for the oars, or they will not match the boat's scale. You can sketch out a plan for your boat on scrap paper to get an idea of the finished size.

1

? **Little Tip:** Take an extra paddle if you're going out in a canoe, kayak, or rowboat.

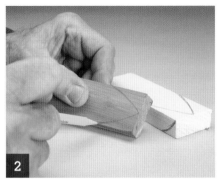

Sketch the outline of the boat on the top of your wood block.

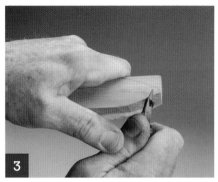

Cut out the prow of the boat, following the lines you just drew.

Sketch the bow on the side of the wood block and cut it out.

Shape the bottom of the hull the whole way around the boat.

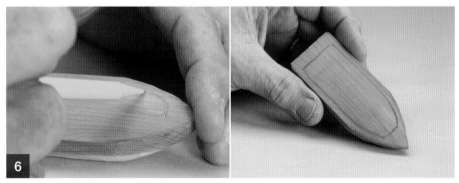

Sketch the interior of the boat on the top of the wood piece.

Using the tip of your blade, cut in around the line you've drawn marking the boat's interior. This is where you should start using the dry dock. If you hold the boat in the palm of your hand, there's a chance you'll slip and carve yourself rather than the inside wall of the hull!

Make a series of V-cuts to remove the wood from the center of the boat, roughly hollowing out the hull.

For the next step, you will need a very small chisel. I made this one from a small screwdriver I picked up at a yard sale. If you don't already have a small chisel of some kind, you can easily make one like mine.

Using your chisel, scoop out the wood in the center of the boat, removing the little slivers you've been making with your knife. Make sure you don't over cut and chisel into the wall of the hull. Note that I've placed a folded rubber band at the front of the boat. This prevents damage as you press the boat against the front of the dry dock while hollowing out its center.

Rowing Your Boat

Going out on the river or the lake? Make sure you're using the right oars. The right oars for you are ones you can hold firmly and you feel comfortable using. If you're a beginner, the oars might feel unwieldy at first, but they should not be so long or so heavy that you can't control your boat. You should be able to submerge the entire blade of oar in the water. If you have to bend or reach down to do this, the oars are too long for you. Go out with an experienced boater so you can practice using different sets of oars until you find the ones best for you.

11

Once you've gotten the inside of the boat as smooth as possible using your chisel, wrap a bit of sandpaper around a little block and sand the interior of the boat, both sides and bottom.

12

Sand the outside of the boat.

13

Measure and cut thin pieces of straight-grained wood scraps to make seats. Glue them into place.

14

Carve the oars from thin, flat, straight-grained wood scraps. If you want, you can make mini-oarlocks for your oars. There are different ways to do this, and I bet you can figure out at least one or two.

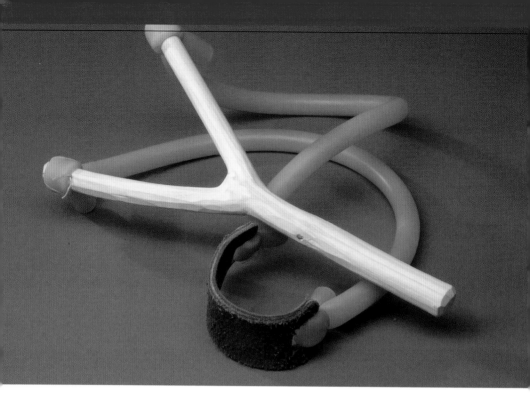

Slingshot

My interest in slingshots came very naturally, as
it also did with bows and arrows, different kinds
of traps, tree houses, and peashooters (except we
made little clay balls to shoot out of our nice, straight
bamboo barrels). Though I'm not proud of all of the
things I did as a kid with my many slingshots, I did do
a lot of fun and useful things, too—like pick way-out-
on-a-limb, impossible-to-reach mangoes!

Of course it was a two-person job. One stood under
the huge, beautiful, ripe mango, and the other stood
off a ways armed with a nice, hard, green guava or
palm nut and a good slingshot. The idea, naturally,
was not to hit the mango itself. That would bruise it
unmercifully. The actual target was the long stem just
above the mango. This being clipped by the speeding
"bullet," the mango would come straight down, into
the hands (hopefully) of the waiting catcher.

MATERIALS LIST

- Knife
- Hardwood fork in a reasonably
  symmetrical Y
- Sandpaper
- Good-quality surgical tubing
- Leather for the pocket
- Dental floss

BIG BOOK OF
WHITTLE FUN

1

Cut the handle of the Y-shaped branch to a comfortable length.

2

Round off the tops of the two top stems of the fork.

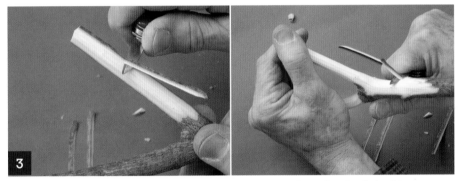

3

For this particular fork, we'll strip all of the bark off. For some of my slingshot forks, I leave on part of the bark, depending on what I want the final fork to look like.

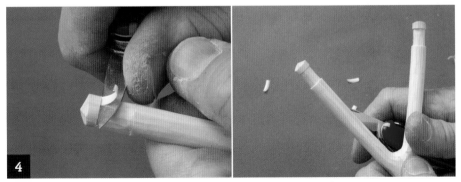

4

Cut a shallow notch around the top of each of the rubber-holding branches.

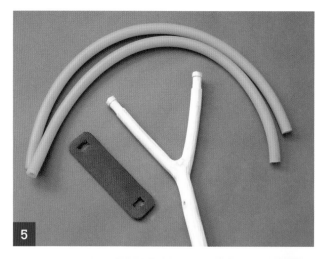

Cut the tubing to the length you want, remembering that you're going to fold the ends around the shallow notches in the two top stems and through the holes you've carefully cut in the piece of leather. When you cut the holes in the leather pouch, make sure you cut very carefully so as not to overcut, thus leaving little cuts that can develop into rips or tears in the leather.

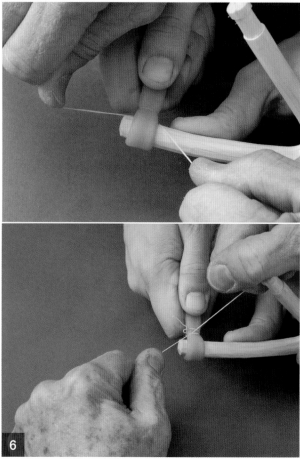

Tying the rubber to the fork is definitely a two-person job. One person holds the fork and stretches the rubber (with the tab on the outside of the fork), and the other person wraps the floss tightly around the stretched rubber tubing and ties it. Don't spare the floss! Double it and use lots. And tie several knots as you go along the wrapping and tying process.

BIG BOOK OF
WHITTLE FUN

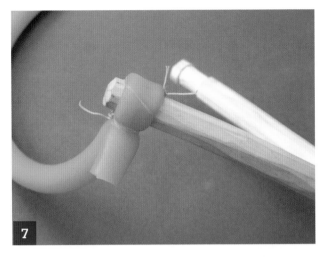

As an extra holding technique, I crisscross the floss several times across the front of the rubber and around the notched stem of the fork.

7

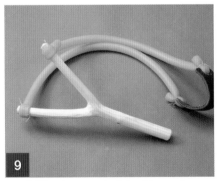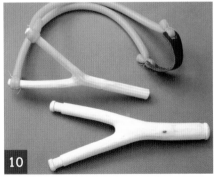

8

Securely tie the tubing to both sides of the leather pouch.

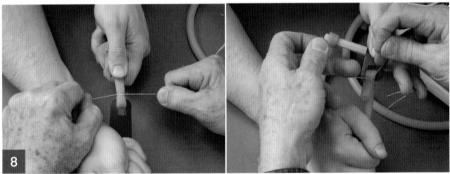

9

10

Done! Slingshots can be lots of fun and very useful, when they're used right. Some states may have special laws and regulations relating to slingshots. Be sure to check before putting yours to use. 'Nuff said.

The particular fork that we used to make this slingshot, while of strong wood, is probably a bit thinner than I would normally use for this heavier gauge surgical tubing. The thicker fork at the bottom would be a better choice.

Checkers

I suspect checkers is pretty much a universal game. I have a huge checkerboard in front of my shop at the Amish Farm and House made from a 6" (150mm)-thick slice of wood from the trunk of a giant American elm tree that once shaded my front yard. Thousands of folks from all over have seen this monster checkerboard, and countless have played on it. I've discovered there are different rules for checker jumping in different parts of the world. Suggestion: Decide what rules you and your opponent will use before you start playing, especially if "flying kings" are involved.

My big table is great where it is, but it's certainly not portable. Here's a good plan for a mini-checker set that can go just about anywhere. As long as you have the sixty-four squares (thirty-two each of two different colors), and two sets of twelve checkers to fit the squares, the size doesn't matter.

MATERIALS LIST

- Knife
- Plywood board
- Straight branch or dowel
- Ruler
- Pencil
- Permanent marker
- Handsaw or pull saw

Little Fact: A checkers game dated from 3000 B.C. was unearthed in Mesopotamia.

Using the ruler and pencil, mark a grid—eight squares by eight squares—on the plywood board. The grid can be as large or as small as you want, just adjust the size of the squares.

Using the tip of your knife, make a slightly angled cut all the way down one side of a grid line. Make a cut at the opposite angle down the other side of the same line. You might have to cut more than once each way for the cuts to meet, forming a v.

Repeat this series of angled cuts for all the lines of the grid. Make sure all the V-shaped grooves are clean.

Color in alternating squares of the board with the permanent marker.

You don't need to do anything complicated or fancy to make the playing pieces. Just use your saw to cut twenty-four little wood slices of the same thickness from the branch. Sand them and color one set of twelve so you can tell them apart.

Tic-Tac-Toe

Many restaurants in which I've eaten have had various versions of peg games for guests (or, more likely, guests' hungry children) to occupy their time while their rib eye and baked potato (and the kids' super-burger and french fries) are being prepared. This particular little tic-tac-toe game project fits that kind of situation very well.

For my own game, I use the back side of the wood slice to make a small woodburned plaque. That way, the piece can serve a decorative purpose while it's not being played. I guess the only catch is to find a safe place for the little pegs, so they don't get lost or eaten by the family dog. I'm sure all of you inventive folks out there will come up with a solution that works.

MATERIALS LIST

- Slice from a seasoned branch about 2–4" (50–100mm) in diameter
- Several straight little twigs
- Pencil
- Ruler
- Handsaw or pull saw
- Sandpaper
- Drill and bits
- Pruning shears
- Woodburner
- Colored permanent markers

Little Fact: "Noughts-and-Crosses" is another name for "Tic-Tac-Toe."

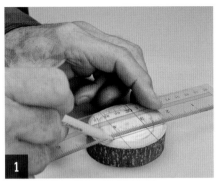

1

Cut a slice of wood from the seasoned branch, and sand it smooth on both sides. Mark the tic-tac-toe grid on one side using a ruler and pencil.

2

Using a saw, cut the lines of the grid. Cut deeply enough that the grid lines are distinguishable, but not too deeply that you risk weakening the wood slice.

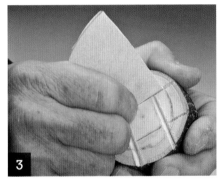

3

Sand the saw grooves clean with a piece of folded sandpaper.

4

Mark the positions of nine holes (one in the center of each grid square) for the little branch pegs.

Never Lose Again

Use the simple strategy of *right, left, above,* and *below* and your tic-tac-toe games will always end in a win or a draw. But careful— for this strategy to work, you must be able to go first. Put your mark in the center of the tic-tac-toe board. After your opponent plays, put your mark in the space to the *right* of his. If you can't, put your mark in the space to the *left*. If that's not available, look at the space *above*, and finally the space *below*. It's the quickest way to become a tic-tac-toe champion.

Carefully drill the holes. Do not go through the slice.

Use wire cutters or a similar tool to cut nine equally sized pegs from a thin branch or twig.

Color one end of each peg with a marker, leaving the other end its natural color.

Using a woodburner and the permanent markers, you can make a mini-plaque out of the piece, using the back of the game. It can hang on a little nail or pin from one of the peg holes on the reverse side.

Ring Toss

This is just a different take on an old, old, old, old game, but the great thing about it is that it's universal. You can play this game with as many people as you want, of any age, almost anywhere you want, and with the rules you pick. You can use the official rules, make up your own, or check out some of the variations that are listed in the box on this page. There's no right or wrong way to play ring toss!

MATERIALS LIST

- Knife
- Several dry branches or sticks
- Drill and bits
- String of choice
- Handsaw or pull saw

Ring Toss Variations

The great thing about ring toss is you can vary and customize it to make it anything you want. The game is portable, so take it to the beach and play on the sand, or make floating stakes so you can play in the pool. If you have a large group playing, set up several stakes instead of just one, and have teams take turns throwing rings at the stakes for a designated amount of time. The team that gets the most ringers (a ring thrown onto a stake) wins.

Cut several pieces of equal size from a dry branch or stick, and drill through the center of each piece. If you cut the pieces from the branch at a bit of an angle, they will fit together more tightly when you make the ring.

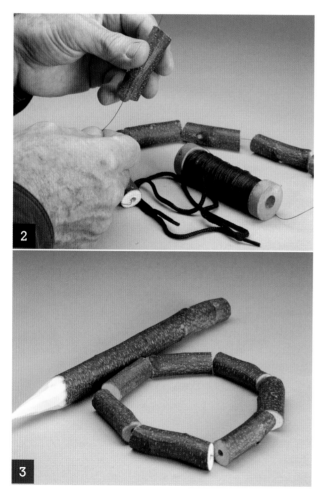

String the pieces together using string, florist's wire, or a shoelace. Repeat the first two steps to make as many rings as you want.

Take another branch of appropriate size and sharpen one end to make a stake. Stick it in your backyard, determine the official scoring rules, and have fun!

BIG BOOK OF
WHITTLE FUN

Pick-Up Sticks

Where and when the game of pick-up sticks was invented, I have no idea. By the time I started playing the game as a kid, the sticks in their various colors came neatly packaged in a little capped tube. The "sticks" were essentially nicely lathed, extra-long, round toothpicks. I can't remember if the game's rules were on a separate sheet rolled up inside the container or if they were printed on the outside of the tube itself.

Somehow I doubt the original game was that refined. I suspect it might have started out closer to the version of literally picking up sticks as we're doing here. These are going to be real sticks that you use to make your own version of the game.

MATERIALS LIST

- Knife
- A collection of straight sticks
- Colored permanent markers (yellow, red, blue, green, and black)

1 Gather a bunch of sticks (more or less straight), five permanent markers (yellow, red, blue, green, and black), and make sure your knife is sharp.

2 Sharpen both ends of each stick. The points should be fairly long and tapered.

3 Color the sharpened ends. Officially, pick-up-sticks has thirty sticks: one black stick (twenty-five points), seven red sticks (ten points each), seven blue sticks (five points each), eight green sticks (two points each), and seven yellow sticks (one point each).

Pick-Up-Sticks

Color	Black	Red	Blue	Green	Yellow
Points	25	10	5	2	1

Set the points needed to win before starting. One player holds the sticks vertically and drops them into a pile. Players then take turns removing sticks from the pile without moving the others. If successful, players get another turn. If a stick moves, play passes to the next person, who may either attempt picking up a stick, or restart play, picking up and dropping the pile again. The player who picks up the black stick may use it to remove sticks; only the black stick can be used this way. If all the sticks in the pile are picked up in one turn, the pile is created again, and play continues until the player loses his turn. Picking up a red, blue, and green stick in order earns players 34 points.

Top

When I lived in Contamana, Peru, I had all kinds of fun with very simple toys like tops, marbles, and bottle caps. Tops of all sizes were used in different games. Though I don't remember where the tops came from, I suspect most were handmade, carved from local hardwoods (like orange, lemon, and guava), with a nail as the point.

I'm sixty-seven as I write this, meaning Peru was fifty-six to fifty-eight years ago. Banking on what I remember of Peruvian rain forest top making, I decided to try making one the way my fellow top throwers did. The following is what I came up with, and it actually worked, which is why I'm sharing it here. When I wound the string around the top and threw it at the floor more or less the way I remember, the little guy spun beautifully! (After a few tries, I should admit.)

MATERIALS LIST

- Knife
- Hardwood branch
- Sandpaper
- Handsaw or pull saw
- Drill and bits
- Screw
- Hacksaw
- File
- Emery cloth
- Wet-or-dry sandpaper (optional)

Little Fact: Did you know there's a Spinning Top and Yo-Yo Museum in Wisconsin?

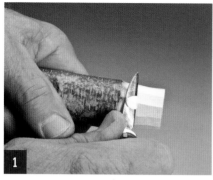

1

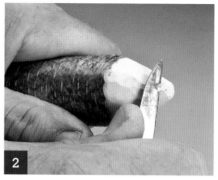

2

Remove the bark from one end of the branch and start shaping the point of the top.

Make sure the point is not too sharp!

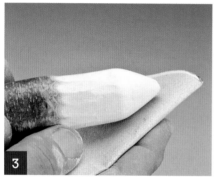

3

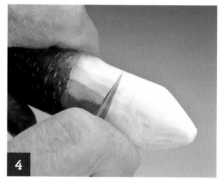

4

Remove some of the bark further back on the branch and sand the top's point smooth.

Mark the other end of the top by making a small cut around the branch.

Dreidel

The dreidel is a Hanukkah toy with four sides and a letter written on each side. In a traditional holiday game, the dreidel is spun and the children guess which letter will be face up after the dreidel falls. The winner gets a prize, usually some kind of food or candy, although the game can be played for any kind of special treat.

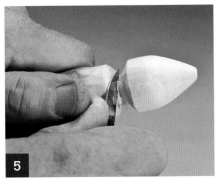

5

Carefully notch around the top of the top, using the previous cut as a guide. Leave a small section connecting the top to the rest of the branch.

6

Cut the top from the branch, cutting through the branch a fraction of an inch above the notch you've made.

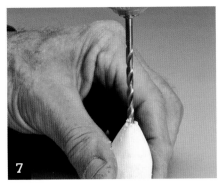

7

Drill a hole in the point of the top.

'Top-Notch' Camping Eggs

Ingredients:

12 eggs

1 lb. (454 g.) bacon

½ cup chopped onion

½ cup chopped pepper

1 tbsp. paprika or cayenne pepper

Shredded cheese

Milk

Directions:

Cut the bacon into small pieces and cook over the fire in a pan. Add chopped vegetables when bacon is about half cooked. Beat eggs in a large bowl and add milk to taste. Add eggs and paprika to the pan and mix with bacon and vegetables. Let mixture cook until eggs are done, stirring often. Sprinkle with cheese and serve.

Tip: Go Greek by substituting the above ingredients with spinach and feta cheese.

Little Fact: Discovered in Malay, the world's largest top weighs in at 15 pounds (6,804 grams).

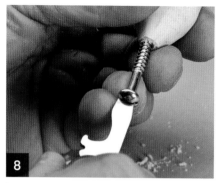

Insert a screw into the drilled hole. Choose a screw that will fit snugly into the top, but not so tightly that it will split it.

Trim away the top piece, leaving only the core extending from the top like a stem.

Trim the stem so only a bit of it is left.

Sand the top.

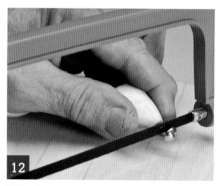

With a hacksaw, saw off the head of the screw.

With a file and some emery cloth, or wet-or-dry sandpaper, round the end of the screw. Once you've finished this step, wind a string around the point of the top and throw it at the floor to make it spin.

BIG BOOK OF
WHITTLE FUN

Rhythm Sticks

Working with branches and wood scraps of all kinds (most of them being hardwoods), I've noticed that totally dry wood pieces of various thicknesses and densities make an array of sounds when hit against each other. Some have a distinct ring, while others produce more of a clapping sound, and some, a deep thud. Some have a high pitch, others low. Where you hold the stick makes a definite difference. Holes drilled in them also affect the sound.

For this project, I collected a variety of branches— different sizes, lengths, shapes, species of wood, etc.—rounded the ends a bit, drilled holes in some, and just started knocking them together in all kinds of different pairings. The variety and range of sounds is amazing!

MATERIALS LIST

- Knife
- A collection of hardwood and softwood branches
- Drill and bits
- Sandpaper

Little Fact: Ridges in a stick will make a new sound if rubbed against something.

Gather a bunch of branches. You can use branches of any shape and size, even forked ones. Generally, I think you'll get better results from harder, denser woods. They'll produce a crisper sound. Of course a good *thud* from a softer wood might add a unique tone to your stick orchestra.

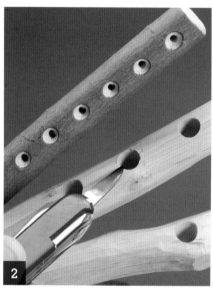

The rest is really up to you. Drill holes of varying sizes into different sticks, experimenting with the different sounds they produce. Smooth the edges of the drilled holes with your knife and sandpaper. You can remove the bark from the sticks and sand them smooth or leave it on.

If two sticks sound particularly good when hit together, you can drill a hole in one end of each stick and tie them together using string. Make sure the string is long enough to enable you to hold one stick in each hand and strike them together. You might want to share your creation with your local school's music teacher!

BIG BOOK OF
WHITTLE FUN

Author's Note

So, there you have them—thirty new things to whittle, carve, or otherwise create with your knife and a few other tools and supplies. While another project or two has popped into my mind lately, I really do think the idea tank is quite empty at this point. Who knows though, maybe I'll have another crazy, idea-poppin' night. Or maybe someone else out there will come up with the sequel to this book! Just get in touch with the great gang at Fox Chapel Publishing.

Index

Acquisition editors: Peg Couch and Alan Giagnocavo
Copy editors: Paul Hambke and Heather Stauffer
Cover and page designer: Jason Deller
Layout designer: Ashley Millhouse
Photographer: Scott Kriner
Associate Editor: Kerri Landis
Developmental Editor: Katie Weeber
Proofreader: Lynda Jo Runkle

Tree Craft
ISBN 978-1-56523-455-0 **$19.95**

The Little Book of Whittling
ISBN 978-1-56523-772-8 **$12.95**

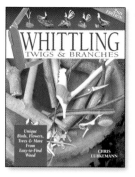

Whittling Twigs & Branches, 2nd Edition
ISBN 978-1-56523-236-5 **$12.95**

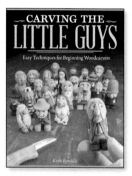

Carving the Little Guys
ISBN 978-1-56523-775-9 **$9.99**

Whittling the Old Sea Captain, Revised Edition
ISBN 978-1-56523-815-2 **$12.99**

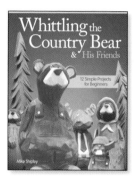

Whittling the Country Bear & His Friends
ISBN 978-1-56523-808-4 **$14.99**

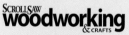

In addition to being a leading source of woodworking books and DVDs, Fox Chapel also publishes two premiere magazines. Released quarterly, each delivers premium projects, expert tips and techniques from today's finest woodworking artists, and in-depth information about the latest tools, equipment, and materials.

Subscribe Today!
Woodcarving Illustrated: 888-506-6630
Scroll Saw Woodworking & Crafts: 888-840-8590
www.FoxChapelPublishing.com

Look for These Books at Your Local Bookstore or Specialty Retailer